About the Author

Angela Canning worked as a secretary for the Hampshire Fire Service in her home town of Winchester, and married Arthur, a senior fire officer.

When they moved to Newbury, they became friends with Louise and Yvonne Veness, who taught them how to run their wildlife hospital for them when they went on holiday. Louise asked Angela if one day she would write their life-story, which she did, and will donate all royalties to a wildlife hospital.

Angela Canning

13/9/21

Wise Owl and Barn Owl

Angela Canning

Wise Owl and Barn Owl

Olympia Publishers
London

www.olympiapublishers.com
OLYMPIA PAPERBACK EDITION

A CIP catalogue record for this title is
available from the British Library.

ISBN: 978-1-78830-966-0

Every effort has been made to fulfil requirements with regards to
reproducing copyright material. The author and publisher will be glad to
rectify any omissions at the earliest opportunity.

First Published in 2021

Olympia Publishers
Tallis House
2 Tallis Street
London
EC4Y 0AB

Printed in Great Britain

Dedication

In memory of my husband, Arthur, and to Julia and Richard.

CHAPTER 1

"Stop that ruddy maniac!" called someone, as a mad driver broke the speed limit in The Strand, screeched on two wheels past a row of vehicles and careered through the traffic lights.

But this was London and who cared? Time meant money. Time meant catching the tube or bus from Aldwych or a taxi from Fleet Street. Time meant buying fashions in Oxford Street or Regent Street, exchanging currency at The Bank of England or The Stock Exchange, racing the great printing presses to roll off the daily news and time for Yvonne and myself, as variety club artists, meant appearing on stage for the evening performance.

Yet in the gutter lay something motionless, something injured. It was a feral pigeon, its right wing bleeding underneath where it had received a gash from the car.

Its orange eyes gazed in bewilderment, its metallic green neck feathers illuminated the white and grey of the rest of its body and as we picked it up, we asked, 'What do we know about doctoring birds?' We knew nothing at all but we also knew we couldn't leave it there.

Nestled into Yvonne's arms, the creature journeyed home with us and once in the kitchen, we bathed its wound gently with a mild disinfectant, gave it a drink and settled it down in a cardboard box with a hot water bottle.

It was six o'clock. Within an hour and a half our public would be awaiting us. We took the underground to Tottenham Court Road and in the dressing room of 'The Scala Theatre', hastily donned our costumes and applied our make-up. Soon the opening music struck up, back came the curtains and we began our double act known as 'The Venices' (a play on our names, Louis and Yvonne Veness). Lithely I performed acrobatics, comic sketches or tap-danced and then as I strummed George Formby songs upon the ukulele, played Country and Western music upon the guitar or accordion, Yvonne sang with her lovely, soprano voice.

What years those were in the 1950s! Tomorrow we were due at Prestatyn for a concert party, the next day at Leicester, then on to Nottingham, York and all over the north of England. We had done it countless times but this time, we took an extra passenger with us, a pigeon living in the van!

Firstly, we had to learn how to feed 'Percy', who refused absolutely and wilfully to eat. We discovered we had to force-feed him and that the only way to give him food was in a paste. Between rehearsals, while Yvonne held him, I administered wild bird food mixed with soaked bread, down the back of his throat. Water had to be given by means of a syringe. It was almost a week that we continued this ritual, when to our immense surprise and relief, Percy began to peck for himself.

But his wound took far longer to respond. If ever he attempted to fly from my hands, his feeble effort always ended in a thud. It obviously hurt him a great deal and we continued to apply Acriflex on a cotton-wool bud, realising that he needed plenty of time.

Percy, meanwhile, became very knowing. Each morning he greeted us with a 'roo-roo' and as I held his warm, soft body, he would cling to my fingers as if they were a twig. It gave us the idea to make a perch for him. At the time, we were traversing the Welsh Valleys and we found a broken bough which we erected in the van. Percy took to this and settled upon it, as if he had used it all his life. He had no objection to the vibration of the engine and was surely, the most travelled pigeon in the whole country!

One morning a month later when we were in Blackpool, we found to our surprise that he wasn't on his bough. We searched everywhere for him amongst all the props and eventually discovered him perched upon a travelling case piled up high in the van. He could fly! We attempted to coax him down and very cautiously he made the effort, taking small lengths at a time. Day by day he became bolder and would fly down for his food. We sensed that he could well fly greater distances if in the open air.

Three days later we returned to London. His wound was healed and we decided to test his reactions. Taking him gently from his box into the greenery of St. James's Park, we threw him up into the air. Percy sensed the joy of freedom, the ecstasy of life in his body, soared briefly in a westerly direction, then changing course, flew southwards over the trees without deliberation until he was out of sight. We watched, both exulted yet sad. We knew we should never see him again.

The next week we were due at 'The Carlton Club' in Nottingham and the next at 'The White Hart' at Thorn, near Doncaster. Being ten years older than Yvonne, I had had more years of experience in showbiz, first of all performing whole-evening treble acts with Percy Swinscoe and Neville King, the ventriloquist, who later became a top artist in The Black and White Minstrel Show. But when I married Yvonne and she wished to join the group, the other two had insisted that they did not want a fourth member, so she and I had decided to 'go it alone'.

Showbiz was a great life and we continued for five years together, performing whole-night acts. Then one day, Yvonne's health began to deteriorate. It seemed as if the hectic life was

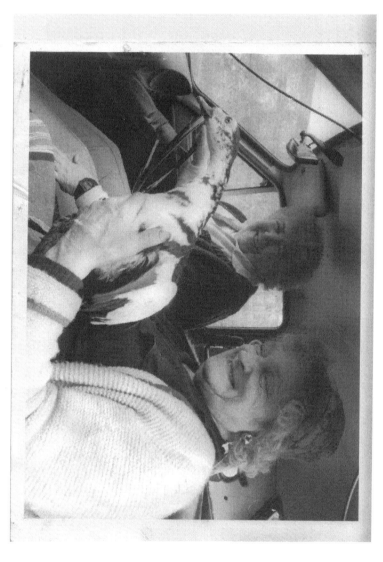

Yvonne at the wheel and Louise with a Muscovy duck on her lap
Photographer: Peter Allen for Farmer's Weekly No. B2214 dated 14/4/83

becoming too much for her and I noticed that she was losing weight. Yet she continued valiantly until several weeks later, when the scales registered an alarming six stone. "Right, to the surgery!" I commanded. The doctor took one look at her over his half-glasses and remarked, "Give up or else!"

It was as if our world had come to an end. But it was our pioneering spirit that carried us through and when Yvonne had fully recovered, we took every job that we could find. The first was running church clubs for Teddy Boys in poverty-stricken parts of London!

And '*sweet are the uses of adversity*', Shakespeare said. With this new life, we first discovered what a priceless thing it is to have time for leisure. We also had time to look after wildlife.

Percy had been the source of inspiration to us. He had shown us that there was a place in this world for the nursing of wild creatures and an idea came to us. Why couldn't we place postcards in shop windows, so that the public could bring us their casualties to care for? We tried it and it worked.

It was in August 1964, when we moved to a new job in the town of Newbury in Berkshire, that we decided to open The Newbury Wildlife Hospital, a thing unheard of. Our white board painted in red, was hung up on the door and announced that we were open day and night and our van was given a headboard to become an 'ambulance'.

To our knowledge it was the first in the country.

CHAPTER 2
1964

'Church House' where we lived, was a solid Victorian building adjoining the parish rooms, with a sizeable garden at the front suitable for our wildlife and it lay along a narrow passage, leading down to the canal.

On the opposite side stood the church dedicated to St. Nicolas, of which I had become the Verger and with its fine perpendicular tower surmounted by pinnacles, dominated the canal and the lock.

Newbury held a cattle and general market on Thursdays and on those days the streets swarmed with country-folk coming in to buy and sell their wares. We were surprised by the doorbell ringing one such morning, to find an elderly man from Aldermaston clutching something which he had brought in his bicycle basket.

"Heard terrible squealing in me fruit cage," he explained, "and found 'e caught up in the netting."

It was a male hedgehog in a pathetic state and I donned some gloves and took it from him. The netting had entwined itself so tightly round his entire body, that it was enough to sever his tiny head and legs. It is nothing for a hedgehog to become caught up in netting or string left around by careless people.

It required two pairs of hands to deal with it and Yvonne and I began by snipping the netting round his neck. But once his head was free, Prickles rolled himself into a tight ball, wrapping his paws around his face. We tried tempting him with pieces of meat held in the direction of his nose but he refused to be coaxed. The little fellow had probably spent several hours in his predicament overnight and was in a severe state of shock.

We achieved little by little with endless patience, snipping each square to remove the cords bound tightly round his legs. They were cut to the bone and we applied Acriflex to heal them, an ointment that is harmless to wildlife if licked. It was then a tricky business to hold them open while we freed his front and even his tiny underparts. Then at last were able to lift the netting from his coat.

Within a trice he had rolled himself into a tight ball again and there was nothing for it but to let him sleep off his shock, in a warm box in a cupboard.

The job had taken us an entire hour!

On the north side of the church, the Kennet was diverted to form a waterfall to work the town flour mill and both sides were a haven for myriads of waterfowl. It was nearing the end of the summer. Swans glided gracefully with their cygnets, now a sludgy white and growing larger week by week, while mallards up-ended, moorhens and coots dabbled in the reeds and tiny dabchicks (or lesser grebes) dived underwater. It was a scene of peace.

Yet for all that, we were beginning to learn that the Kennet was also a hazardous place for unsuspecting wildlife. Careless anglers would leave their tackle behind and a boy came to us one afternoon, in a flurried state.

"A swan by the bridge has a fishing hook lodged in its throat!"

I followed him along the towpath to the spot where it was and my heart missed a beat. It was a cygnet, still with its parents.

Swans with their mighty wing joints and heavy bones are capable of drowning a man and I was aware that the situation was precarious, to say the least. A male swan when fighting, will seize its opponent by the back of the neck. This hold will cause its attacker to collapse and this is what I had to do now. Summoning all my courage, I managed to lure the distressed creature to the bank and with one dart, grabbed its neck and pulled it out of the river to the accompaniment of vicious hissings and imminent attack of the parent birds. Then, as swiftly as I dared, I eased the hook out and returned their offspring to them. Sweet success! Suddenly, loud cheers echoed from all directions around me and I looked up. An appreciative audience had gathered on the opposite bank and on the bridge to watch!

It was a repetition of the old familiar ring of the night-club days but this time hopefully, there would be no encore.

***

The canal was a pleasant place for a stroll in the evening and we made it our regular exercise. It was there that we first met Fluffy, the miller's big black cat, lurking for mice. Fluffy consistently rubbed himself round our legs, enjoying the fuss. He would walk with us as far as the two quaint weavers' cottages, for Newbury had once been a rich, woollen town and every citizen had made a living off the sheep's back. At that point, Fluffy would come no further and we would cross the iron bridge to wander back towards the lock.

On the opposite side stood another tall, old flour mill but now disused and between that and the lock-keeper's cottage, was a piece of waste ground containing some stables and a peacock wandering around amongst the overgrown vegetation.

One evening in late October, a heap of empty fish boxes had also arrived at the scene. "Strange horses, living on fish," we remarked and our curiosity got the better of us. We climbed over the fence and took an unauthorised peep inside the stables. A hundred or more ferret-like creatures stared at us from individual cages, their glossy dark fur tinged with blue.

"A mink farm!" Yvonne announced without hesitation and feeling sickened, we departed on our way.

From the lock-keeper's cottage came the sound of hammering and we guessed he was busy repairing his rowing boats, which he hired out on The Wharf. John Gould even owned the two motor-launches, 'Kelston' and 'Limpley Stoke', which sailed up and down the canal taking the public on joyrides. At the sound of our approach, Buffer, his Jack Russell, came running out to meet us with a series of 'woofs'.

His master stopped his work and came out also, ever eager for someone to chat to. A unique man, tall and thin, with a thirst for open-air life, he was always a mine of information and we commented on the quantity of fish for the mink.

"Oh yes, they're blue mink. Mink were introduced into this country from America in about 1929, you know. Their natural habitat is riverbanks and fens, so that's why their food is mainly fish, although their eyesight under water is poor. In the wild they will also kill poultry if they have a mind to and even rabbits."

As he continued talking, a team of bellringers suddenly commenced their weekly practice and the great stone edifice of St. Nicolas standing opposite us in the sunset, sprang to life.

"I often think what a fine church that is. Have you heard of Jack O'Newbury? He built it. His real name was John Winchcombe, the richest wool merchant we ever had. Even entertained the king and all his court at his house up the road.

Still there now."

"Which king?"

"Henry VIII. Jack felt the old church wasn't large enough, so he pulled it down and paid to have this one built. Can't imagine that today, can you? The churchyard was far larger in past centuries, of course. Even extended to the south…"

"Wait a moment!" we interrupted. "That's where Church House is now. We must be living amongst the dead!"

He threw back his head and gave a roar of laughter. "They won't rise up now after all these years." He returned to his work chuckling to himself and called, "Although they might do tonight. It's Hallowe'en."

***

Late in the night, an eerie sound awoke us from our sleep. It wasn't spirits but a ring of the front doorbell. We seized our dressing gowns, went downstairs and a young couple called, "We've brought a barn owl with a broken wing." We unlocked the door and took the patient from them. It was a beautiful bird, its dark brown eyes glimmering from a heart-shaped face, its white underparts and face glowing a ghostly white. It was obvious why some folk call them 'The White Owl'.

We thanked them and put Barny to bed but as soon as daylight dawned, we knew we would have to mend that wing before it became set. We needed advice and telephoned Peter Scott at Slimbridge. His reply was that he did not look after injured birds! Who were we to turn to? There was no one.

We had to teach ourselves and so we did, by trial and error. It was broken between the 'shoulder' and the 'elbow' and being a large species of bird, we guessed it would take eight to twelve weeks to mend.

We held the wing in its natural flight position and taking a lolly stick, sliced it lengthways down the centre to make two splints. Then we applied one to the topside of the wing and the other parallel to it, to the underside. In those days Micropore had not been invented, but we bound them round with a reel of thin Elastoplast half-an-inch wide, taking care not to splint the wing at the elbow itself, for it would have restricted its flight. We realised that any splint must only reach as far as the bend.

Next, we mended his individual feathers, firstly by separating the barbs and then binding them again with Elastoplast firmly round each shaft, then smoothed the barbs back to their natural position.

It seemed to work and day by day, Barny's confidence began to return. but getting him to eat was a different matter. When we left his meat, diced, in a row along his perch, he always left it untouched. We tried force-feeding him but just as we thought he had digested it, each time he regurgitated it all and we were back to square one. We began to learn Lesson One. It is impossible to force-feed a barn owl.

His natural diet would have been voles and mice covered in fur and we had an idea. We decided to go to the butcher's to acquire a rabbit skin. Then we cut it up, rolled it carefully around each piece of stewing steak and left it on his perch. It did the trick! Next morning his food had gone.

We continued to perform this ritual methodically every night but alas, the next week there was a crisis. "No rabbits have been brought in this week," the butcher told us, attired in his striped apron. "I'm sorry."

Once more we were in despair. Barny refused to eat again.

In the evening we took our usual stroll along the canal.

Fluffy, the miller's cat prowling outside, ran towards us, rubbing himself round our legs in the usual greeting.

"You're moulting, Fluffy," we said, as countless hairs were distributed over our slacks.

"Fluffy, you're the answer!" I exclaimed suddenly. "Allow me a handful of your beautiful fur."

I pulled it out gently and took it back home; then wrapping each piece of meat in the black ball of fluff, we left it along Barny's perch. In the morning, Fluffy's fur lay tossed on the ground but the meat had gone.

CHAPTER 3
1965

Spring arrived, the time when nature is alive with productivity—
"And the time," Yvonne declared, "when her products all find
their way to our hospital!"

Boxes of nestlings and fledglings began arriving, some left
in the emergency cages in the garden when we were out. Most of
the contents bore no resemblance to their parents at all. Little,
brown fledglings with spotted breasts and brown beaks were
blackbirds, curious, grey fledglings without a hint of speckles
were starlings, tiny, speckled, brown balls of fluff represented
robins, while some were unattractive, little, bald specimens
without a hint of feathers at all. To keep them protected, we put
the nestlings in boxes in the warmth of the airing cupboard (well
ventilated) and the fledglings in cages in the spare bedroom.

It is nature's miracle the way the mother senses that the
climate is right to lay and incubate her eggs, so that her young
are hatched at the exact time to feed upon emerging caterpillars,
grubs or insects. But the job had now been handed over to us! We
had to find a substitute, something as moist as the natural food
softened by the parents' saliva. Tiny gaping mouths waited in all
directions from six in the morning until dusk, the nestlings
demanding theirs every two hours and the fledglings every four.
But it was an impossible task to find enough insects. We mixed
chick-crumb with raw egg and in desperation, gave them morsels
of tinned cat food. But it was not adequate. Only half were

surviving and we were burying sad, little corpses.

"What did the doctor have to say?" asked Yvonne one day, as we wiped our brows, perplexed.

"The doctor?"

"…who wrote that book that we found in the Charing Cross Road."

"Oh!" I recalled the book that she meant. It was one we had found one day in London while browsing in the dusty alcoves of the Dickensian bookshops, a small, illustrated book, its pages yellowed with age. I searched around and found it. It was entitled:

BRITISH BIRDS

Their Successful Management in Captivity

with

Other Allied Information for Fanciers

Published 1891

Birdcage Walk in London is a living memorial to the poor, wild, birds snared and caged in those days. Linnet Terrace in Cambridgeshire is yet another, built in 1904 from the proceeds of selling linnets at a penny each. It was quite deplorable, yet the information which Dr J. Denham Bradburn had collected on the care of them was invaluable. I read the piece about feeding on page twelve:

"Here's something. '*Mealworms:—the larvae of a beetle which thrives in large flour mills.*' Perhaps the miller could help us? '*The beetles can be kept in large jars, fed on oat or barley meal and will lay their eggs on sacking.*'" I stopped. "Oh, that's no good. '*They should not be disturbed for three months or so.*' We need something immediately." I read on. "What about Gentles, the larvae of the blow-fly? It seems they can be produced very quickly, although the doctor didn't want anything to do with it. He says '*All you need do is, hang up any offal and you will soon meet with your reward—plenty of maggots and plenty of filth and smells.*'"

"Well, we needn't hang it up. We could bury it," Yvonne ventured.

"Yes, we could," I agreed, wondering why I hadn't thought of it. "Come along then. Let's see what Mr. Liddiard on the bridge has to offer."

"You could try tripe," he volunteered, pushing his straw boater to the back of his head, "or there's some pig's liver about to be thrown out."

"We'll take it," we said thanking him. We packed it all in our bag and returned home.

We lay it out on the earth just below the topsoil, covering it speedily. I fancied it was already beginning to smell which could only have been my imagination, in anticipation of the joys to come. Next day we uncovered it. It was seething with white maggots and we filled a polythene box with the wriggling things.

A pair of tweezers made a marvellous substitute for the parent's beak and the fledgling blackbirds never failed to amuse us. Each one, when about to take a tweezerful or three or more, always gave a hearty 'chirrup'. The starlings, the Squawkies, however, gaped their mouths open wide as soon as they saw it but snapped them shut before the food was inside. It was a work of art to get it in and when in, unless we pushed it to the backs of their throats, it was never swallowed. Usually, they would have the tweezers in their beaks, then would shake their heads and the food would fly everywhere.

A syringe did not prove an easy method by which to administer water, so we hit on the idea of giving them the chick-crumb soaked in water on the broad end of a nailfile.

The tiny pied wagtails and bluetits, each about two-and-a-half inches long, were a far greater task. They refused to open their beaks, like minute pins and there was only one way—to prise them open gently from the side and force-feed them.

The maggots had proved to be the answer but if we did not use them up within a week, they became stiff and still and began pupating. Then every single one of our charges refused point-blank to touch them! The answer was to keep them in a ventilated, polythene box in the refrigerator.

At length, a cheeky starling plus two of the blackbirds began to feed themselves from a dish, the food flying everywhere and it was amusing to watch them. We had had them for two-and-a-half weeks and we knew they would show us when they were sufficiently matured to go.

Meanwhile, the number of waterfowl in trouble on the river was increasing quite alarmingly. Not only were fishing hooks caught round the heads or legs of swans and ducks but reports were coming to us, of a practice in fashion by young hooligans. They would seize a duck, fasten a rubber band around its bill and the back of its head, preventing the poor creature from opening its mouth and so it would die of starvation.

When a duck was terrorised, it was impossible to catch it on the bank. One day we had to borrow one of the lock-keeper's boats to row after one and rescue it. It was no easy matter chasing a duck up and down-river, in an attempt to lasso it with a large fishing net. Ducks are wonderful fliers and it meant getting John Gould to open the lock-gates and swing-bridge. Even then, the poor thing, flapping its wings desperately, raced away escaping us.

Still the fledgling season was not over and we never

expected to receive our next patient—a baby kingfisher. He was a source of delight. Even as a fledgling his colours were beautiful and his metallic blue-green led us to name him Sapphire. The problem was to find ways of feeding him and there was nothing for it but to set off armed with a fishing-net and a jam-jar down to the river. We soon became expert minnowers!

After two weeks, he began to fly small distances and we decided to provide a miniature pond for him in his pen, which we filled with the minnows. Sapphire loved it. We watched him diving from his little bough and catching them himself, first tossing them into the air, then swallowing them head-first.

When a month had passed by, his wings and tail were mature and when we discovered his under-beak was turning red, we discovered that Sapphire was a female! Her senses were keen and we decided, sadly, that we must take the gamble to see if she could cope with the big world outside. We knew a protected tree-lined spot along the bank of the canal at Speen Moors, took her there and set her free. Sapphire perched on a low, over-hanging bough of a willow tree, watching the current uncertainly.

For what seemed an eternity, she did nothing and then, eventually disappeared amongst the foliage. An hour later we returned to see if she was adapting to her natural habitat but she had completely gone. For days afterwards we searched for her again, but Sapphire was enjoying her new life, nowhere to be seen.

It was months later, in August, as we were taking a stroll along that part of the canal, that a sudden streak of electric blue skimmed up-river and we were ninety per cent sure that it was Sapphire. She had shown us that she was a true creature of the wild again and gave us a sense of reward.

We made our way home. How was it, we asked each other

as we walked, that with their tropical colours, kingfishers ever came to be a native of our isles and left willing to endure with us the ice of winter, freezing to their bough? It was a wonder of nature.

The miniature pond that we had provided for Sapphire in her pen proved advantageous whenever we had tiny, orphan ducklings or cygnets to nurse. But the trouble was, we had no large pond for injured waterfowl like swans, Canada geese or ducks. We had thought about making one for some time and had acquired a strong P.V.C. liner from a garden centre, resistant to claws. Now it required a search through an instructional gardening book, to learn the 'do's' and 'don'ts' of pond-building.

It was mid-day and a there was a knock at the door. It was interesting to note how we came to know a complete cross-section of the public in our new venture, from the richest to the poorest. Around Newbury are many landed estates and this time it was Lady Porchester from the Highclere estate, whose father-in-law was the sixth Earl of Carnarvon.

She had come to ask for advice. "I've a pet quail," she told us. (Quails' eggs are a sought-after delicacy for the table.) "There is nothing wrong with her wings, but she will not fly."

"Quails always live and feed on the ground," we explained. "They are very secretive creatures, hidden amongst crops on farmlands and normally only fly when disturbed by sportsmen or predators. They are known as 'bottom feeders'."

She laughed at the term. "I see. Thank you so much for your help," and drove off.

A week later she returned with an injured drake. "I spotted this poor thing by our lake. You see it has a broken leg. Could you please look after it?"

"Of course," we said. "We'll mend the leg and would you

mind if we release him again on your estate, once he's better? Whenever possible we like to return our patients to where they were found."

"Any time you wish," she replied and left a donation for his keep.

Yvonne took him, naming him Charlie. He was a handsome mallard with the characteristic iridescent green head, changing to purple in a different light. As the drakes mature, so their colours become brighter and Charlie's bill was a vivid yellow, which indicated that he was at least two years old. Yet his poor orange leg hung limply.

"I'll see to him," she said and disappeared into the kitchen.

I remained in the garden, to begin making a hole for the pond in the cool of the evening. I dug and dug, but soon learned that it wasn't easy-going. The ground could not have been touched for years and the soil was rock hard...

Charlie's leg was broken in the place most common, I thought as I worked, just below the 'knee joint' and being a large bird like Barny, it would take eight to twelve weeks to mend. He seemed quite fearless of humans. Maybe families on the estate or grounds men had been used to feeding him. He would enjoy swimming on his pond while recuperating...

I continued digging. Yvonne was expert at first aid. I knew she would use lollypop sticks again, invaluable when mending legs of large birds and this time she would bind them with a roll of two-inch Elastoplast to each side of the leg, (definitely not to the front and back so that the poor bird couldn't move)—and at least a quarter of an inch above the foot and a quarter of an inch below the knee joint.

I continued, perspiring...

Being a waterfowl of course, she would then take a sheet of

waterproof, green oil skin from the chemist, (the sort mother used to use over lint to cover our cut knees as children) and cut it into strips to cover her work. Charlie could then swim to his heart's content, all the while that his leg was mending.

Phew, what hot work it was...!

Suddenly, my spade hit against something hard. I dug further and unearthed two objects.

Yvonne was still in the kitchen, obviously having taken a liking to Charlie. She was talking to him as I waltzed in, wiping my brow, and asked, "Good heavens, what have you got there?"

"Have a guess."

She took them from me and scrutinised them, removing the soil. "It can't be! Yes... it's a pair of brass, coffin handles!"

CHAPTER 4
1966

It was the beginning of July and a van drew up in the road. Out stepped a man in uniform, walked down the alleyway and rang deftly at the doorbell.

"Good morning! I'm Brian Sanders, the new RSPCA Inspector. I have heard all about your hospital. Have you room for an eagle owl?"

He produced a cage covered over with a blanket and we peered underneath. Blinking nervously at the daylight, was the tiniest of baby owls, the size of a tennis ball.

"Oh, a Little Owl. That'll be our first one!"

"That's Bob," he announced jovially. "Every time I look at him, he bobs up and down."

"Well, would you and Bob like to come in?"

The man stepped inside. He was tall and thin with brown curly hair and in no time, had settled himself on a stool in the kitchen, sipping a mug of tea and chatting amiably. It appeared that he was straight out of college. Amongst other things, he owned no less than three bulldogs and his hobby was riding around on a motorbike, the dogs accompanying him in the sidecar! We also loved dogs and had quite a discussion about them.

"How did you dream up the idea to run a wildlife hospital?" he asked at last, putting down his mug. "First one I've ever heard of. Mind if I look round?"

"Feel free."

We showed him the patients that were recuperating, those in intensive care in dark, confined spaces and the newly made pond. He was obviously impressed.

"As you see, we're acquiring so many patients, we have scarcely enough cages!"

"What you really need is an aviary, isn't it?" he replied thoughtfully, then suddenly took an urgent look at his watch. "Oh, good heavens, I'm due at Thatcham ten minutes ago. Be seeing you!" and he went rushing off.

We did see him again and with his enthusiasm and dedication, he became an ever-ready help.

Meanwhile, Bobby had been put into a cage in a dark corner to acclimatise to his new surroundings. He could only have been barely five weeks old and being an orphan, remained huddled, his yellow eyes looking lost and miserable.

"What does the doctor have to say about you?" I asked, flicking over the yellowed pages of the book. I came to the one headed: 'Little or French Owls'.

"Feed on rabbit or chopped raw beef at nightfall."

We administered a drink of lacto, the mother substitute, lest he was dehydrated and hand-fed him on finely minced beef suitable for a fledgling.

The following day, Bobby's eyes looked a little brighter and he ventured to move along his perch. Within a week, he had perked up considerably. From a shy, retiring, little fledgling he began to grow into a cheeky juvenile, each day becoming bolder. Upon seeing us at six o'clock in the morning administering the breakfast round, he would start bobbing up and down at our approach, his yellow eyes now as bright as buttons and giving a shrill, excited, 'kee-kee-kee-kee', 'kee-kee-kee-kee'.

"Good morning, Bobby," we would greet him and he would hold out his head to be tickled.

Next morning, we were busy and forgot to acknowledge him and to our amusement, he sat in the corner, head held down and sulked! We discovered, if we did not acknowledge him each morning afterwards, he did the same!

Meanwhile, crises were still occurring on the fast-flowing Kennet. From West Mills where we lived, the river flowed under the barrel-vaulted bridge in the main street and on to the Wharf, where large groups of waterfowl resided. When a message came that a swan was caught up in the rushes near the police station, Inspector Brian was the first to the rescue.

He and I borrowed one of the lock-keeper's clinker-built boats moored at the Wharf and rowed steadily round to the back of the police station, amazed to see huge trout slithering in and out of the reeds.

"The dream of any angler," Brian remarked, pulling at the oars and then added, "I say, this boat's leaking. I'm getting wet. Are you?"

I was decidedly and it didn't feel too comfortable but there was no time to worry about things like that, for in a large clump of rushes that bordered the bank, there was the swan.

"It's a cob, too," I hissed. "Look at the size of its neck!"

Our plan of attack was to row to the bank as quietly and unobtrusively as possible. Then, while Brian held back the rushes, my task was to approach it from the left, make a dash for the back of its neck with my left hand and grasp it so that my right arm was wrapped firmly round its wings. Brian would then disentangle its feet.

We neared it stealthily and were poised ready, when suddenly the swan was alerted. Already in a terrified state, it became even more aggressive than normal as it sensed our presence. With a flap of its mighty wings, the boat capsised and we were sent sprawling into the water, wetter than before!

'Kee-kee-kee-kee, Kee-kee-kee-kee', called Bobby, as he detected my squelching footsteps returning along the alleyway and I sensed it might even have been a laugh.

***

Injured animals were brought to us at any time of the day or night and when the doorbell rang at dusk one evening, we were presented with a baby pipistrelle bat.

The tiny thing was no more than two-and-a-quarter inches long and had a torn wing membrane. We prised open its microscopic mouth and gave it a drink of lacto. Then, knowing bats are cold-blooded, we worked swiftly and hammered together a wooden bat-box, which we hung up high outside, where Batty could recover from its ordeal. There it hung, upside down by its tiny feet!

Next evening, we fed it with chopped insects that had been hovering around the window and pieces of maggots, on the pointed end of a nail file but afterwards, Batty returned to its original position, upside down, as pathetic as before. It was impossible for it to fly and we knew it was only our intuition which could ever enable it to do so. Somehow, we had to mend that wing.

We needed something as weightless as the tiny, woollen creature itself and we scratched our heads. Should we use muslin—or maybe tulle? Then Yvonne had an idea. She remembered that up in the loft was a pair of black, very fine denier stockings kept from our theatrical days. In a trice she disappeared up there and searched for them. Soon she returned triumphantly, then cut a piece large enough to cover the tear, with at least three-quarters of an inch to spare to extend round it.

Now we needed three splints cut to the length of his veins, to hold the nylon on either side of the tear, then down the centre. But what could we use that would be light enough? We decided on balsa wood.

The next problem was, what to use to secure them? We hit on invisible Sellotape.

We pulled Batty's wing out gently, looking in wonderment at the way its tiny claws were attached so perfectly to the ends. Then very carefully and gently we worked, covering every aspect of the jagged tear and secured the Sellotape over the edges of the wing, so that no ends would penetrate to adhere to any foreign object.

The job was finished and we held the wing to the light. There were no gaps where air could get through—a VERY important point to ensure and we returned Batty to its box to rest. Once again it hung upside down and fell asleep, oblivious of the world about it.

We continued to administer its feed to it every evening, hoping that the wing would heal. Batty took its time and we couldn't believe our joy when three weeks later, after feeding, we noticed that he was attempting to unfold them. One night, as it balanced itself upon my hand in the usual way, it flapped them cautiously.

"Look!" I cried. "It's trying to fly!"

Suddenly, as if making the final decision, Batty flitted away silently into the dusk.

'Kee-kee-kee-kee!' called Bobby, joining in the excitement. A good dinner had just flown past his cage.

In September, Brian called again. "My Bobby, how you've grown!" he said, looking into his cage.

'T'wit, T'wit,' replied Bobby, bobbing up and down.

"That's his normal conversation," we explained. "The kee-kee-kee-kee is reserved for exciting occasions, like when he hears our footsteps in the alleyway."

This morning Brian was not in uniform as he was on holiday, and he asked, "How about coming outside and being introduced to my mate, then?"

We followed him to where his motorbike was parked. Peering out from the sidecar, was the large frame of a bulldog. "Meet Caesar, the gentle giant." Out bounded a panting and wheezing fifty-two-pound hulk, his flat face slobbering in greeting. "His sisters, Jane and Cleo, are back home," he added.

"Good gracious," I remarked, slapping and tickling Caesar affectionately, "what on earth do you feed them all on?"

"Between them they get through three pounds of meat a day, mixed with biscuits. But you have to be careful not to let them put on *too* much weight."

We led them both inside.

"I'd love a dog," Yvonne announced enviously, as she put the kettle on.

"Any particular sort?" Brian asked, as he sat down, with Caesar drooling over his feet.

"The sublime to the ridiculous. It has to be a Peke," I volunteered with a wink. "I don't suppose the RSPCA would have one?"

Yvonne filled the pot and poured a bowlful for Caesar as well. Caesar lapped his up noisily, slopping half on to the floor.

"I'm afraid not. People don't normally abandon Pekes, but I'll find out who breeds them if you like and give you a ring."

Brian, as usual, was as good as his word. There was a breeder just a mile away called Lisa Grey, who happened to have a litter born on the 26th July.

We went to see her. 'Deepnell Cottage' was set back from the road opposite 'The Swan' at Newtown. We rang the bell and the door was opened to reveal a small, plump lady who took us through to her kennels. Adorable, little bodies jumped up excitedly as we passed, their flat noses squashed against the wires. In the end one, six healthy bundles of fluff no bigger than kittens, confronted us with their mother.

"Come along now, Eno," announced Lisa Grey kindly. "Let us see you."

She scooped up one, explaining, "How do you like this one? He hasn't been reserved yet."

She thrust the silky, black bundle into Yvonne's arms.

"He's simply gorgeous!" she gasped, being licked to death by a wet tongue.

"We'll take him," we said, without hesitation. When we came away, we had his pedigree and instructions on his care and feed.

Bobby began his shrill call as soon as he heard us returning.

'Yap yap!' responded Eno in surprise.

'Kee-kee-kee-kee to you!' answered Bobby, bobbing up and down as he saw him.

"Meet 'Enops Satire of Deepnell'," we said to Bobby, "or rather, Eno. Eno has come to his new home."

Autumn dawned and under cover of its beautiful tints, we were to learn that there is always the annual horrific slaughter. This year, it was inevitable again. Pheasants, rooks and woodpigeons became the victims of 'sportsmen' and even protected species were shot in error. The maimed found their way to our hospital and our cages became overloaded.

One evening at dusk, another noble lady came to our door.

'Kee-kee-kee-kee,' called Bobby shrilly, as I opened it.

"Good evening," a voice said sweetly. "My name is Lady Craven. Please could you look after this tawny owl for me?"

The Craven Estate was at Hamstead Marshall, five miles to the north-west of Newbury.

"Like you, I love wildlife," she explained, "and no shooting is ever allowed on my estate. But I found this owl on the perimeter along the Enborne Road."

"Certainly," we replied and thanked her.

The gunshot wound beneath the wing had torn it an inch from the poor creature's body. We cleaned it gently with Acriflex, removed the visible pellets and then taped it back in its natural position.

We found owls the most appealing of creatures and wondered whether this one was a male or a female, for in the Tawny, the sexes are the same colour. All at once, I remembered a game which we used to play as children. We simply dangled a plain, gold ring on a piece of cotton over an animal or a fertilised chicken's egg and if it began to swing like a pendulum it was a male and if in a circle, a female.

I fetched a ring and tried it over our new patient. It 'thought' for a second or two, then gradually began to swing very steadily, then quite forcefully, in a circle.

"We'll name her Bess," I said.

It was time for Bess to be retired to a usual dark, confined corner for intensive care patients, to prevent movement and to enable her to recover quietly from her injury.

Some nights later, the telephone rang and woke us from our sleep. A couple at Bucklebury were watching over a fox that they had found shot in a wooded area near their cottage and asked if we would fetch it.

We dressed swiftly and started up the 'ambulance'.

"Oh dear, that's disturbed Bobby," Yvonne said, as his excited chattering began again. "Be quiet, you naughty boy! You'll wake the whole neighbourhood!"

We proceeded on our way. The cottage was situated out in the wilds and we found it, with some difficulty. The poor animal was in distress and we motored home, with Yvonne nursing it on her lap.

Having parked the van in its usual place near the church, we walked up the alleyway. An uncanny stillness hung in the air at the hour of two in the morning.

"There's something wrong," I said suddenly. "Bobby isn't calling."

"He must have heard us," Yvonne remarked, in a puzzled tone.

We deposited our patient swiftly in the warmth of the kitchen before attending to it and went outside to look at his cage.

There was silence, not even the flap of wings and we shone a torch inside. Upon the ground of his cage lay his little body motionless and I opened the door and took him in my hands. His grey and white flecked feathers were intact and there was no evidence anywhere of an intruder's entry into his cage. The wire was untouched.

Yet Bobby was dead.

***

John Gould was fixing a wooden seat on 'Kelston', his thirty-foot motor launch, early in the morning, and stopped when he heard the news.

"I'll come over," he said at once, and examined the sad, little bundle of feathers.

"That's a mink."

"A *mink*?"

"Yes, that's what done it. He separated the feathers at the back of Bobby's neck. "Just look here."

At the base of the skull was a bite which we had not seen in the darkness.

"Mink attack their prey at the back of the neck like other members of the weasel family. Then they suck its blood. One of them must have escaped from the farm."

"But there's no sign of where it could have got in."

"It would have squeezed under the wire. You see, it's not pinned to the ground."

He looked over to the other side of the canal. "I suppose it's living along the bank somewhere. You know, I've watched those mink gnawing a hole in their cage for a whole week until they can get out. I've warned the butcher many times. He owns them."

As we buried Bobby in the garden with tears in our eyes, we planted a Forsythia shrub where he lay.

CHAPTER 5
1967

When March arrived, the blossoms burst forth smiling, as golden as the spring sun. Bobby's spirit was alive and with us, as bright as he had always been.

The strange thing was that little Eno always chose that shrub to lie under, panting, after he had been scampering around, as if he knew it was something special. He was a cute, little chap and had grown to three-quarters of his full size. He would trot around with us inquisitively and dancing on his back legs, to see into the cages as we performed our rounds.

The spring approached and by May we were immersed with the usual boxes of nestlings and fledglings in their numbers and we worked tirelessly. The strong survived and the weak succumbed but it was a well-rewarding task. Yet not only did the feathered creatures find their way to us but a surprising number of other things and when one morning, Brian Sanders popped his head round the unlocked door and called, "Anyone at home?" he had brought a little, white kid.

"Someone found her tethered in a lane starving. She was left by gypsies. As you see she only has one teat. I said I thought I knew someone who would take her," he ventured apologetically, "although I know you're a Wildlife Hospital…"

"Bring her in," we chorused.

The little animal's ribs were like a greyhound's, her spirit downcast.

"Come along, Lucy," I said without thinking, giving her a huge bowl of milk, plus apples and carrots which she munched hungrily and then I attempted to comb her matted hair.

When Brian had departed, we put her to roam freely in the garden and at night made her a comfortable bed of straw in the shed.

After a week or two, we were pleased to see that her coat was becoming healthy again, as a Saanen's should be and her body was gradually putting on flesh. Also, we thought she was happy and she didn't take long to prove it. Each morning as we opened her shed door, she bounded out, leaping around like a springbok, as skittish as young goats are.

We became attached to her and every day we took her for walks with us, over the swing bridge and back past the lock, so that she could get her natural food, leaves and plants. There, she always met John Gould with Buffer, who made a fuss of her and she would chomp away happily, pruning his rosebushes.

But one day Lucy went missing. We searched for her everywhere in the garden but she was nowhere to be seen and we became worried. An hour passed and a telephone call came from a shop owner to say that she was down Northbrook Street, the main street of Newbury, in the busy road!

We hurried down and fetched her, bringing her back on a lead and put her in the garden again. But once Lucy had savoured the delights of the wide world outside, she found the grass on the other side greener.

One day, John Gould rang the doorbell. "Look who I've found outside Woolworth's," he announced. It was Lucy, attached to a piece of string.

"Whatever can we *do* with you, Lucy?" gasped Yvonne, her hands on her hips. "We've only just mended that fence!" We didn't want to keep her tethered.

John had a paddock and a good high fence and an idea crept through my mind. I knew he had an eye for Lucy and I ventured, "Would *you* like her?"

The thought had not occurred to him and he considered for a moment. "Well now, what would *you* say, Buffer?"

Buffer looked up and gave a 'woof' of approval. The matter had been decided.

And so, Lucy went to live at the lock-keeper's cottage, where all the passers-by got to know her and would offer her a titbit from their lunch. It became common even, to see John walking down the town with her on a lead, or to the vet to have her hooves trimmed, as is the proper care of goats. Not a soul batted an eyelid.

The Rector of St. Nicolas' Church also knew her well and one Christmas a request came for her to take part in the forthcoming Nativity Play. Would she mind standing by the crib? Lucy had no objection and played her part so well, that she could have won an Oscar.

Years later we heard that Lucy had died. She had lived to the age of sixteen and because she had been associated with holy matters, the Rev. Chris Savage buried her solemnly in the churchyard.

***

Meanwhile, Brian called again and as he sipped his mug of tea with Eno on his lap, he remarked, "What about that aviary? Don't you think it's about time you had one? You have room in the back garden."

We looked at him surprised. Aviaries were expensive and he

well knew that our pin money was needed for feed and medical care of the patients.

"We should need at least £50," I commented.

He winked. "I might know where I can find it."

"Are you going to do a robbery?"

"Maybe." He held back his head, giving a chuckle and depositing Eno on the floor, departed to his next call, so that we forgot all about it.

The next newcomer was a feral pigeon. We had many pigeons to care for but this one was so identical to Percy with his orange eyes, metallic, green neck feathers and white and grey of the rest of his body, that we named him Percy II. We did not know that Percy II was to become as special as the first.

Brian turned up two weeks later and to our surprise, had a letter in his pocket. We tore it open. Inside was a cheque for £50 (worth £500 today)!

"We'll have that aviary up in no time," he said. "Better get planning permission."

It took us just three weeks to obtain it from the Council and we were ready to go. Brian arrived with the materials—cement, posts, netting, wood, varnish, nails, screws, hinges and lock— enough to build an aviary twenty feet in length and twelve feet wide. We got to work that very day.

With great enthusiasm, we set the posts in concrete. When sufficiently firm, we secured the netting all round. At the weekend we began building the partitions, double doors and lastly made a good, strong roof. It was a marvellous job and took up the whole of the back garden. It had taken the three of us a fortnight to build.

It happened to be September and excitement reigned in the town. This month there was to be a Newbury Festival Week, a week that purported to be crammed with events, terminating in a carnival.

A coachload was expected to join in the celebrations from Newbury's twin-town of Braunfels and in their honour, a German Biergarten had been arranged in Victoria Park, accompanied by lusty beer-drinking songs played from the bandstand.

On the opening day, Sunday the 17th, there was to be a concert in the Corn Exchange given by The Newbury Festival Concert Orchestra and The Newbury Operatic Society. During the week there would be shows, dances and exhibitions, a Pop Music Competition in the Corn Exchange judged by the well-known radio disc jockey, Tony Blackburn, while throughout the Friday night a four-hundred-and-fifty-pound ox would begin to roast on a spit in the Market Square, to be ready to be partaken of by all, next day at the Carnival.

To rule over all the proceedings there would be a Festival Queen. She would be chosen from amongst the local, pretty girls at a grand ball to be held in The Plaza on the 7th and two of the judges would be the well-known Newbury radio star, Basil Jones, who played John Tregorran in The Archers and Neil McCullum, of BBC TV's 'Vendetta'.

When the evening of the ball arrived, the band struck up the opening music and the atmosphere was electric. Twelve lovely finalists lined up before the jury to be chosen 'for their personality, grace, beauty and ability to converse'. The winner was selected at last. It was twenty-year-old Christine Jones, a hotel receptionist at 'The Chequers' and amidst great applause, the Mayor, Councillor Christopher Hall, placed the crown on her head.

Christine's first engagement would be to attend The Newbury Agricultural Show the day before the festival began, to host functions throughout the week, to assist Tony Blackburn with the judging of The Pop Music Festival on the Tuesday and her last, to ride in honour in a 1913 Lancaster car at The Newbury Carnival.

And on Monday the 18th, her duty was to open our aviary! The aviary stood smart and ready, a white ribbon hung across its double-doors, while shrubs and trees containing roosting boxes decorated the edges. It looked a treat and a credit to Brian's intuition.

The awaited day proved warm and sunny. At two o'clock, a crowd comprising Brian and Betty, his wife, the Chairman of the RSPCA Fundraising Committee, several RSPCA members, John Gould, our neighbours, friends and a host of onlookers, together with a reporter from The Newbury Weekly News, waited expectantly. Christine had been spotted rounding the church in the official car.

She stepped out, the sun illuminating her beautiful, blonde hair piled high upon her head and enhancing her bright, blue sash, worn from her shoulder, bearing the title 'Newbury Festival Queen'. Elegantly she walked towards the hospital, shook hands with us with a smile and we led her to the back garden.

"My goodness, it's magnificent!" she exclaimed upon seeing the aviary. Ceremoniously she cut the ribbon and announced that it was officially open. Everyone cheered and bottles of champagne were popped.

"Would you like to see round the hospital?" we asked and then prevailed upon her to perform the honour of releasing Percy II, who was now ready to go. She took him delightedly in her hands. Percy II, apprehensive at first, gave a quiet 'roo-roo', in his affectionate way as she spoke to him, then balancing himself on the palm of her hand, made his departure, soaring into the air and alighting on the church roof. Then, as if considering what to do, he took off, circling in the air and flew away.

On the Thursday, it came about that Percy II was given a special mention along with our hospital, in a five-and-a-half-inch column on the festival page in The Newbury Weekly News.

CHAPTER 6
1968

The patients at the Wildlife Hospital took to their aviary as ducks had taken to the pond. Rooks, crows, magpies and pigeons to name a few, poured in during April and May and amongst them was a nest of blackbirds, whose beautiful song at dawn was a treat to hear. The earthen floor of the aviary around which they all pottered before learning to fly, served as a ready means of exercise and acclimatisation, before returning to the great world outside.

A gentle song thrush with a wounded leg was amongst them and we called her Laura. We loved to watch her, her beautiful spotted breast ranging from cream to buttermilk. She would hop along the ground listening attentively, her head cocked on one side, then quick as lightning, would stab at the earth and pull up a worm. Sometimes she discovered a snail amongst the foliage, which she would thrash against a stone, retrieving the contents from the broken shell. As soon as she recovered from her injury, we released her.

At the weekend came two orphaned Tawny owls, brought by a young boy. "Their nest was destroyed," he told us. "I can't keep them because I have to go back to boarding school. You will take care of Woo and Wol for me, won't you?"

His little face looked so dejected that I said reassuringly, "Of course, son. Now you go back to school and you'll have no need to worry at all."

We put Woo and Wol, hardly a month old, into a roosting box and they nestled together on their perch, blinking at their new surroundings.

When Brian called upon us one day, owls and kestrels watched suspiciously from the trees in the aviary, cheeky magpies and jackdaws sprang amongst the foliage, while the host of fledglings trilled from the boxes in the end partition. He talked to them animatedly, seeming satisfied with his handiwork. Suddenly we heard him calling, "Look!" and went to where he was standing. A thrush was returning with worms and pushing them through the netting into tiny gaping mouths, feeding all and sundry!

"That must be Laura," we exclaimed, "fulfilling her mother instincts!"

We had seen it all before. A fledgling blackbird that we had reared, only just able to peck itself, had been feeding the three others in that same aviary!

Meanwhile Woo and Wol were thriving well, growing day by day. It was always heartening to observe patients surviving to maturity and we wished it for these two more than any other, as they were the pets of the young boy.

Spring turned into summer, when running a wildlife hospital never ceased to be without its surprises. We answered the doorbell at seven one evening and there stood a lady clutching a heron.

"I've brought it all the way from Scotland."

"*Scotland*?"

"I was returning from holiday and found it on the Clyde, covered in oil."

"Well, it's great to know that there are caring people about like you," we answered and took it from her.

Thank goodness it had obviously not swallowed too much oil, or it would never have survived the journey and there was hope of saving it. Swiftly we administered vitamins through a funnel with a long tube obtained from the vet's, knowing it would be dehydrated.

Our next task was to set about removing the clinging, black grease first and foremost from the parts which it would try to preen. We worked and worked on its plumage, rubbing Swarfega into its wings and breast and immersing it after each stage, in washing-up liquid and hot water. Finally, we rubbed liquid paraffin into its feathers to restore their natural oils.

Next, we cleaned its long legs and razor-sharp beak, nature's weapon to spear its prey while standing in the river. In normal circumstances, we would never have been able to do this. In the wild if you do not approach a heron delicately and as quick as lightning grab its neck, it will slash you or even blind you. But Archie was weak and hadn't the will to protect himself.

After several days, he began to recover his dignity again and in the typical way of fish-eating birds, took a herring which we threw to him, seizing it in the centre of its body, lifting his head and turning it round to eat it head-first so that he would not choke.

One day, I went into his cage and startled him. Archie regurgitated his food whole on to the ground, giving me as much of a surprise as he had had. We learned so much simply from watching wildlife close at hand. This was the characteristic of herons!

It was time to take our usual stroll with Eno along the canal. We had not gone far, when an Alsatian pup came bounding up to us asking for fuss and we stopped. His mistress was following behind with a little girl and a baby in a buggy. We patted the puppy's light brown head enhanced by a black 'V' and he placed his paw in my hand.

"How do you do. What's your name, then?" I asked.

"That's Rusty," volunteered the little girl.

"And how old is he?"

"Twelve weeks," answered her mother. "But I'm afraid we can't keep him any longer. He's jealous of the new baby, you see. It's terrible."

"Oh dear—and have you found another home for him?"

She shook her head. "We've asked everywhere but it isn't easy homing a dog that has a temperament. He has one more week or else…" she added worriedly.

I looked at Rusty's pleading eyes, begging for his life.

"Give us your telephone number," I said. "If we hear of anybody, we'll let you know."

That night, for some reason, I could not get that dog out of my mind. I tossed and turned until Yvonne woke up.

"Whatever's the matter?"

"That pup. His pleading expression keeps coming back to me."

"But what can you do about it?"

"We *could* have two dogs, couldn't we?"

She sat up, incredulous. "A Pekinese and an *Alsatian*?"

I ignored the remark. "Didn't *you* think he was a lovely dog?"

"He was gorgeous."

"What's wrong then?"

"I thought someone once spoke about going from the sublime to the ridiculous…"

We collected Rusty the next day and brought him home.

There didn't seem to be any problem with him getting on with a Pekinese. They both took to each other like long lost pals, chasing around the house and garden (being severely admonished if they disturbed the wildlife) and afterwards, would lie down exhausted together in Rusty's dog-bed.

Although Eno was the senior by two years, it was he who decided when they had had enough rest. He would lick Rusty impetuously round his face and having incited him to start playing again, put his head inside his mouth!

Each evening, as soon as the word 'walk' was mentioned and collars and leads were fastened on, Eno would pick up Rusty's lead and pull him out of the door!

Watching the two was always a comedy and one day we had an idea. To earn some extra money, we put an advert in 'The Newbury Weekly News'.

Dog Owners,
Why not join in the fun
and bring your pet to

DOG TRAINING CLASSES
Every Monday Evening,
7.30 p.m.—9 p.m.
at
St. Nicolas' Church Hall,
West Mills, Newbury
2/6d. per session

For this, we always provided a free cup of tea and people turned up with dogs of all shapes and sizes. There were mongrels—a Retriever—there was Digger, a Redsetter who constantly dug up his master's vegetable bed—("Quite uncontrollable," he told us); a lady brought along Josephone, a black Cocker Spaniel, who was quiet and quite the opposite; two Jack Russells arrived, who frolicked and tumbled over one another; a Dachshund stood snootily ignoring the rest; there were three Labradors and a Dobermann, who turned out to be as gentle as he looked fierce.

Eno and Rusty regarded all these intruders with surprise and curiosity, thinking it a wonderful opportunity to have a game and nosed their new-found friends in delight.

"Right now," I called, clapping my hands to get attention above all the commotion, when all were assembled in the hall. "Let's begin with some obedience training."

The first exercise was spent teaching the dogs to halt and then return to their owners; the second, encouraging them to guard a basket or their owner's gloves at the door of a 'shop'. (Two chairs placed apart served the purpose.) Both exercises created a great deal of amusement. Most of the dogs spent their time doing exactly the opposite but the star of the show was Josephine. She performed all her duties to perfection.

The next week we played at 'scenting'. Each owner had been asked to bring along his pet's toy. All the dogs were then shut outside in the passage and the toys were placed together in the centre of the room. Then, they were all let in together. Digger bounded for his spotted ball called 'Measles', while a Jack Russell charged in and out of his legs and sent him sprawling; a Labrador had hold of one end of a slipper and the Retriever the other, both tugging, barking and squealing; Rusty seized a one-eared teddy which didn't belong to him and charged off with it, with Eno at his heels, while a mongrel sat with a pink rabbit in his mouth, growling at Josephine and daring her to touch it.

They were happy and we were happy. But there is a saying that happiness is a fleeting thing. In the midst of it, suddenly misfortune struck and the reason was one that no one would have expected.

Ever since we had left London, I had felt my body was beginning to suffer a sex-change. I had ignored it for years, but its progression suddenly developed beyond control and I knew I had to succumb to it. I decided to dress as a woman and change my name from Louis to Louise Veness, while Yvonne and I agreed that we would become known as the Veness Sisters.

In those days, this condition was scorned by the Medical Association and I received no help whatsoever.

It was also scorned by St. Nicolas' Church where I was the Verger. The position was always held by a man and we were given notice.

As we sat devastated by the canal on that sad summer's evening, its grand edifice loomed majestically over the water and the mill stood silently in the glow of the setting sun. The forty-foot launch, 'Limpley Stoke' was returning through the lock and John waved from the helm as he passed, ferrying a crowd of holidaymakers back home. He had not heard the news.

We watched the swallows and martins circling and sweeping over the water after insects. Within a month, they too, would be returning to a warmer land and the summer would be over.

Without The Wildlife Hospital, who would fare for their young, born late in the year, the fledglings too immature to fly across the mammoth seas to South Africa and left behind, to face the cruelty of winter?

How could we desert them? The words of Kipling suddenly ran through my mind.

'If you can force your heart and nerve and sinew
To serve your turn long after they are gone;
And so hold on when there is nothing in you
Except the will which says to them, 'Hold on!''

"Yours is the earth and everything that's in it…" Yvonne continued.

"Well, isn't that us?" I asked.

"I suppose so."

"We've won before and we'll win again!" I vowed.

And as always, we did.

CHAPTER 7
1968/9

It would be surprising how many tales the River Kennet could tell of centuries past, as it ran through the town of Newbury. Since 1810, of course, it had been converted into The Kennet and Avon Canal, yet it was nonetheless a site of antiquity.

As we sat by the river that August evening, we noticed that one of the shops numbered 17 West Mills, comprising two buildings, was unoccupied.

"How about seeing if we could rent it and sell antiques?" Yvonne suggested out of the blue.

I wondered why I hadn't thought of the idea myself. How often we had spent many a happy hour at Petticoat Lane or the Portobello Road, browsing through the antique stalls, returning with many a treasure.

But we had to find out who the landlords were. We guessed John Gould would know and he did. The premises belonged to the Surveyor in Cheap Street, Alan Seward. So, off we set the next day and requested the key. Our enthusiasm increased upon looking round the premises. There were fifteen rooms in all, plus a piece of ground to the rear which would be suitable for our wildlife. Accordingly, we applied to The Newbury District Council for permission to open a shop.

But we were stunned by the reply. 'We are sorry. The canal is not a suitable site for antiques.'

What a lot of nonsense! I penned a letter to The Ministry of the Environment at Bristol and in no time, an energetic, little man was sent down to inspect the premises, who had no hesitation in giving his decision that 'the canal lent itself ideally to the sale of antiques'.

And so, we moved all our furniture into the abundance of rooms, when this time the Council informed us that the premises were condemned and were not to be used for living in! What was it that they had against us? We sensed the reason. They did not approve of our wildlife.

It seemed as if the odds were against us, but never to be outdone, we wondered if one of the large estate owners might have a cottage which we could inhabit and at the same time, run the shop. I decided to write a letter to each one. A reply came by return of mail. It bore an armorial crest and was from The Countess of Craven.

"Dear Miss Veness,

Thank you for your letter, and I am very sorry to hear of your situation.

I should like to offer you one of my cottages
on Irish Hill on the road to Kintbury and if you
wish, you could house your wildlife in the grounds.
Would you care to call and see me tomorrow
morning for coffee at eleven o'clock?
Yours sincerely,
Signed: Elizabeth Craven

The immense Craven Estate of three hundred thousand acres, was situated four miles west of Newbury. The beautiful landscape with the River Kennet running through it, was purchased by the 1st Earl of Craven and 13th Viscount Uffington in 1620.

The great manor house which he built resembling

Heidelberg Castle, had been burnt down in the early eighteenth century, so the family had then extended their hunting lodge and moved into it. It was there, in 1963, just five years ago that the 6th Earl of Craven had died tragically of leukaemia at the age of forty-seven, leaving the present Countess with three young children.

Three years later, Lady Craven had married her loyal Estate Manager, Kenneth Banner and they had moved into a newly built Dower House nearby.

The day after we received the letter, we made our way to the Enborne Road and turning off, drove up a private avenue leading to a gateway bearing the family crest and surmounted by figures of griffins. Before us stood the splendid white manor house, 'Hamstead Lodge', which they now let as a nursing home and following the road curving to the right, we reached the Dower House and rang the bell.

It was opened by the butler who ushered us into the sizeable saloon. Lady Craven soon appeared, slim and attractive, with sapphire blue eyes.

"I am sorry to say that since writing to you, I have received a disappointment," she began. "An old lady lives in the cottage adjoining the one which we had in mind for you and she has expressed a wish not to have her peace disturbed. It is a delicate situation. You see, her husband was killed by a tractor while working on our estate and she has been granted the right to live in the cottage for the rest of her life. Have we anywhere else where the sisters could live, dear?" she asked, as a pleasant man with ruddy complexion entered the room. It was Kenneth Banner, who came and sat with us.

"There are only the four cottages at Enborne which I intend to bulldoze at some time."

"Oh yes, the disused cottages on Luckes' Farm. An authoress was the last person to occupy one until her death but it wouldn't be habitable now." She considered for a moment and then an idea dawned. "What about the residential caravan? Couldn't we make a present of it to them?"

"I don't see why not," her husband replied. "They could park it on the green in front of the cottages and if they wished, use them to shelter their animals."

Yvonne and I looked at each other in surprise and expressed our gratitude.

"I will take them to see the caravan," he offered and finished his coffee.

The cream caravan was parked a short distance down the road. We looked over it. It was twenty-two feet in length, fully carpeted and appointed with everything but linen and cooking utensils. It was a gift from heaven.

All we needed to do, was to tow it to the site.

Our life at Enborne turned out to be something quite unique. The site lay in the centre of Luckes' Farm and after walking over farm fields, we reached the four Georgian cottages, which were now hidden behind a hopeless mass of overgrown gardens. The green stretching in front of them was of a good size but the problem was, there was no water, electricity or toilets. We guessed the cottages must have had some form of water supply and we decided to look around.

A dilapidated elm fence enclosed the gardens. I climbed over it first and suddenly found the ground giving way beneath my feet. Clutching wildly at the fence, I pulled aside the long grass upon recovering and discovered an uncovered well. Bodies of dead rats and rabbits were floating deep down in the water!

Without any hesitation we searched around and found a

piece of corrugated iron and some heavy stones with which to cover it up.

On walking back to the farmhouse, we came across the farmer himself, hat on head, busily engaged in milking his Hereford herd.

"Hello!" he called. Then, in sudden recognition, paused from his work and came over, holding out a large hand. He was a plump, jolly man and his broad face beamed. "I'm Cyril Luckes. You must be the ladies coming to live on the green…? Sure, tap's over there," and pointing to it, offered us the use of it any time we wished.

We thanked him and once out of earshot, Yvonne held her sides laughing. "What a character! Did you see what he was sitting on, doing the milking?"

"No."

"A Chippendale chair!"

Towing the caravan to the site was beyond us. It was a test of ingenuity and the only way was to make a detour. We employed a man in Newbury with a Land Rover and paid him £5 to perform the operation, which he achieved by fighting his way through narrow lanes and finally mountaineering a railway bank. He returned home a ball of sweat, declaring he had earned it.

Having dismantled the aviary and cages, we finally moved on Yvonne's birthday, the 30th August and arrived at night, Rusty and Eno accompanying us. As we opened the caravan and began making up the beds, the dogs chased around wildly outside, obviously excited at their new surroundings. Every so often, an impetuous barking echoed from Rusty, who had found something to sniff at around the cottages.

"Just look at him. He's going mad!" cried Yvonne, looking out of the window.

The outbuildings of the cottages possessed low sloping roofs and Rusty was on his hind legs, about to spring up on to the end one. As he achieved it, his barking became even louder and using it as a springboard, he leaped on to the cottage roof where the slates had slipped off, his body quivering, his hackles up. Suddenly he seized a rat as it ran along the bare rafters.

Eno was waiting at the bottom expectantly, as Rusty descended with a tail hanging out of his mouth.

The night passed without disturbance and six o'clock arrived the next morning, time to fetch water. Taking two buckets apiece, we set off over the three farm fields.

Cyril Luckes was up early, washing down his milking parlour and stopped while we stood waiting as the water rushed into the buckets. In chatting, we discovered that he had an interest in antiques. Obviously, not only did he possess his priceless milking stool but had a set of old masters stored up in his loft. We wondered if they had reached the same fate of nonentity as the Chippendale chair.

We were soon to learn that everyone in the village knew him. Not only was he chairman of the Parish Council but a governor of the little Enborne School, a warden at the church and every Sunday afternoon he waved to all and sundry, as he cantered round the lanes upon a hunter as well built as he was, taking his weekend exercise.

We staggered back home, the water slopping in the buckets. We supplied it to the dogs, boiled some for our own needs and as soon as we had breakfasted, decided to explore the cottages. We put our shoulders to the door of the first. It heaved open with a jerk, surprising a heap of empty bottles which descended to the ground. As we ventured into each of the rooms, we were met with even more. They had contained Whisky and Gin. I remarked that if this was the one the authoress lived in, I wondered she wasn't too sozzled to write.

The cottage, as we expected, was in a sad state of neglect and so was each of the others. However, we worked all morning clearing them out and afterwards, went into town to fetch some of the patients, including Woo and Wol plus Archie, the heron, taking care to strap his beak and wings, so that he would not hurt himself in transport and installed them in their new abode.

The weekend after our arrival at Enborne, a Land Rover pulled up along the road and out stepped the tweed-clad figure of Kenneth Banner. "Good morning," he called. "Lady Craven wondered if you would like to come and have a cup of coffee and meet the children?"

We said we should be delighted and at eleven o'clock made our way to the Dower House. In the saloon, three little figures, free from their schooling, stood up and shook hands politely. Thomas, the heir, was a tall, slim, lad and announced that everyone called him Humphry. The younger boy, Simon, with brown, wavy hair the colour of his brother's, gave a pleasant smile of welcome, while their little sister, Anne, too shy to speak, stood demurely by her mother.

Coffee was brought to the huge, round table in the centre and Lady Craven asked chattily how we and the patients were settling in at the farm. "The children are very interested in wildlife," she continued. "Would you mind if they came to see your patients some time?"

We looked at their eager faces. "We are going to set our heron free this weekend," we replied. "Would you like to come with us and watch?"

"The lake in the parkland would be a good spot," Kenneth Banner volunteered. "I have seen herons there from time to time."

"The lake's by the river," Humphry explained. "We'll show you if you would like us to, Miss Veness."

We said the place sounded ideal and that afternoon, all three children clambered into the van, eyeing Archie's cage curiously.

Around us stretched acres of woods, park and farmland and after wending our way for a quarter of a mile, the scenic lake lay before us. An immense number of waterfowl was performing upon it. Graceful mute swans glided along slowly, their large bodies reflected in the water. Coots squabbled in the reed-beds, moorhens emerged and disappeared again, tiny dabchicks dived and bobbed up again after a full minute, while a host of mallard ducks, upon seeing the children, swam over and scrabbled on to the land, quacking greedily for food. Humphry and Simon had brought a bag of bread and bent feeding them, little Anne begging to be included.

As soon as they had finished, I opened Archie's cage and took him out, holding him firmly by the back of the neck. Gasps of wonder came from the children. "Just look at his long legs… and look at his black crest!"

"Ah, but do you see his beak?" I asked. "It's razor-sharp so that he can spear his fish. Never touch that."

"Shall we let him go?" Humphry asked at last.

"Yes," I agreed. "Come on, Archie," and released him.

Archie seemed nervous, then suddenly, sniffing the fresh air, took off, flapping his wings heavily, and with legs outstretched behind him, propelled himself like an aeroplane over the water into the island of trees opposite. We waited some while, watching him through the leaves, as still as ever.

"Do you think he will show us how he catches a fish?" Simon asked hopefully.

2 patients at the hospital
Picture by David Hartley

"He'll need a little time first, to adjust to his new surroundings."

"May we come and see your hospital tomorrow?"

"Come and watch us giving them their breakfast," Yvonne said.

The children did, eager to help. By now we had brought several more patients out to Enborne and ecstatically, they administered seeds and nuts to the small birds and left large cubes of steak on the perches for the hawks and owls. Next, Humphry busied himself breaking up loaves of bread for the swans and ducks, while Anne, overcoming her shyness, begged to help give a baby rabbit her bottle of lacto.

Simon stood staring at the sleepy owls in wonderment. "I love Woo and Wol," he said, "and I'm going to christen the two other Tawnies 'Snoozy' and 'Snooty'."

"We had a newcomer yesterday," we told them. "A badger. She was injured on the road." Inspector Brian had brought her out to us.

It was a signal for them all to rush into the second cottage to look. Badger was taking her daytime nap, her handsome black and white, striped head tucked into her body.

"Her leg's strapped up!" Simon exclaimed.

"Yes, it was broken. We've put it in a splint."

"Could you show us how to mend legs?"

"Certainly, we will."

Very quietly, they slipped her plate of apples, meat and grain in through the aperture in her cage for when she woke up, refilled her bowl with water and crept away.

The children were to become regular visitors.

***

We had stocked the shop with our own items of bric-a-brac as a means of starting up and as we had insufficient money to purchase antiques directly, we advertised in the local paper, offering to sell items for commission in the shop.

The telephone rang as soon as the paper came out and our first caller asked, "I have a grandfather clock for sale. Could you sell it for £7?"

We fetched it in our van and as we were unloading it, an onlooker called, "I'll give you £16 for that," and the clock had gone!

After that time, we sold many grandfather clocks, mostly to Americans who took them back home and no doubt re-sold them for many times more. I often reflect on how sad it is that half of England, together with London Bridge, is on the other side of the Atlantic.

We found that rummaging amongst jumble sales or even Steptoe's yards, revealed pieces of value and one day we discovered a large, metal dragon in a deplorable state of verdigris. We brought it home, used half-a-tin of Brasso on it and an even larger amount of elbow grease. It polished up so well and was such a good saleable attraction, that it did not take any time for a dealer to spot it.

"Good heavens, you shouldn't have polished that!" was his reaction. "That's bronze!"

One only cleans bronze with hot, soapy water!

In those days, there was no Arthur Negus to educate folk into taking a second look at grandmother's piece of china or to turn out their attics for heirlooms. We were by no means connoisseurs either but we were to learn by experience and experiences were many!

The door opened and in came a lady, unwrapping a small object. "Could you sell this for me for £5?"

I took it from her. It was a milk jug with nothing attractive to offer it. "Well, I'll try," I replied dubiously and when she had gone out, remarked to Yvonne, "We'll never get £5 for *that*."

I had not had it for ten minutes before a man came in and asked how much we wanted for "that little jug in the window?". I took it out.

"Do you know what this is?" he asked and handled it lovingly. "This is Old Lowestoft. The spout is a sparrow beak and it's a very rare piece. These were only made for fifteen years. You could have asked anything you liked for it!"

He was the curator of a museum!

One day, we were given an old oil painting to sell, upon which one could just discern a harbour in Venice. It was gloomy and unappealing and we stood it on a table.

"How much do you want for that?" asked a customer with a cigar in his mouth.

"£50."

The man handed over the money and took it away without quibbling. Shortly afterwards, he invited us to come and see it. He had had the picture cleaned, erected a light over it and it was transformed to beauty. It was by an Italian master.

But the prize story was the portrait of a water spaniel, which we hung together with others on the wall. A lady browsing round the shop stopped suddenly and singled it out.

"£60," we asked of her.

Obviously, the sort of lady able to buy whatever took her eye, she did not hesitate.

It was by sheer chance two years later that we bumped into her housekeeper in the street, who had since left her employ. "Do you remember that painting of a dog which Mrs. B. bought from you? She sold it, you know, at Sotheby's for several thousand pounds. What do you think it was?"

We waited curiously. "No idea."

"A Stubbs!"

We laugh when we think about it now but at the time, we were making enough money to feed our wildlife and that was all we really asked.

Then one terrible day, misfortune struck. We arrived to open up the shop and were shattered to find a policeman waiting there. "There has been a burglary," he said apologetically. The lock had been forced and we looked around in tears. Every room had been ransacked.

As the months crept on, our shop became a target for even more robberies, one after the other. We became hopelessly in debt and had no capital to buy any more stock. Then, it seemed as if we were quite miraculously saved by our guardian angel and we were able to carry on.

The telephone rang and a voice asked, "I am leaving the country and would like to clear my house. Could you come and have a look at it?" It was a lady who lived in the town.

We arrived and couldn't believe our eyes. Every room resembled an Aladdin's Cave.

"We're sorry, dear," we said to her. "We just haven't that kind of money. You'll have to ask somebody else."

"But I want *you* to have it," she insisted, surprisingly. "I have a love of wildlife and I don't want more than £30 for the lot."

We looked at each other. One piece alone was a Dresden oil lamp, surrounded with porcelain flowers and surmounted by a white bowl. It was exquisite and alone was worth more than the sum she was asking for the whole house.

But the lady was adamant, so we loaded up our van. That collection was sufficient to settle our debts and to keep us going for six months.

We were returning home early from the shop one Friday afternoon when Kenneth Banner stopped his Land Rover, about to pull into the drive and asked, "Care to join us for a cup of tea?"

We thanked him and followed him up the avenue of elms. Lady Craven welcomed us, as gracious as ever but as she poured us each a cup, we sensed that there was something on her mind.

"We must thank you for putting up with the children so often," she said. "They love to see your hospital."

Kenneth Banner passed the plate of fruit cake. "Children are a problem today, aren't they?" he remarked, voicing his thoughts aloud. "In these so-called 'liberated' sixties, there are so many bad influences to corrupt them, don't you think...? Drugs, promiscuity, violence, street demos. It makes bringing them up a headache instead of a pleasure."

"I believe Louise and Yvonne have had quite a lot of dealings with young people," Lady Craven stated, before we could reply.

"Have you really?" he asked, sugaring his tea. "Tell us about them."

We related how we had run the church clubs for poor boys, to take them off the streets of London. "There were lads who were frightened and browbeaten, to those who were tough Teddy Boys," we assured them, "but we got them all interested in sports and competing for cups. By teaching them the right way, they usually developed into responsible adults."

"That is why we consider it essential to encourage our children in worthwhile occupations," Lady Craven added. "We like them to visit your hospital to learn how to become caring. Simon, in particular, is simply fascinated by your owls."

"Well, we hope to set two Tawnies free just before dark," I replied, having decided that Woo and Wol were ready to go. "Do you think they would like to join us before supper?"

That evening we called for the children, who were waiting eagerly.

Before we departed, Simon stood gazing into their cage and talking to them. "Do they have to go?" he asked sadly. "They're my favourites, Woo and Wol."

"You can't keep them forever, you twit!" called big brother, Humphry. "Come on. Get in."

We drove to the edge of the woods upon the estate, darkness beginning to fall already. Leaving the car, we took out the cage carefully and the five of us walked a distance along the tree-lined track. Twigs cracked under our feet and the wind shivered through the branches.

"It's a bit spooky," commented Humphry. "You'd better hold my hand, Anne."

"Here's a nice, large oak tree," Yvonne announced at last, sensing the massive form. "How about here?"

We put the cage down and opened it but nothing stirred.

"Come along," the children called softly but there was no response. Woo and Wol refused to go.

"I expect they like the hospital too much," said Anne.

Simon put leather gloves on and lifted Woo out, who clung to his fingers. Then, taking him to the lowest branch of the oak, he coaxed him on to it. Woo stayed there for some minutes and eventually, hopped into the shelter of a higher branch.

Suddenly, by sheer chance, the hoot of an owl quavered from the heart of the woods and Wol, as if by magic, flew out deftly from his cage into the oak and became lost in the foliage.

"Do you think they will be all right?" the children asked

anxiously, after we had waited a little while.

"We will make sure. We'll come again tomorrow morning to see if they have gone."

We turned back.

"Yesterday evening I saw a barn owl returning with a mouse in its claws, to the stable clock tower," Simon announced importantly as we walked home. "When I'm grown-up, I'd simply love to make a wildlife park here. Do you think you could help me, Miss Louise and Yvonne?"

Next morning, being a Saturday, we walked with the children back again through the woods. As we neared the oak tree, a great disturbance was coming from that direction. Rooks were flying around cawing loudly and mobbing something in it which they obviously regarded as a predator.

We hurried towards the tree and clapped our hands, shooing them away. Then, looking up into the leaves, we could see two creatures huddled together miserably on a bough, awakened from their day-time doze.

"It's Woo and Wol!" the children cried at once. "Oh dear!!"

I called to them and whistled and to everyone's surprise, they both flew deftly from the bough towards us and alighted on my arms!

We fetched the emergency cage from the van and took them back to their sanctuary. Woo and Wol were happy once again— and so was Simon.

The spring brought the rains. The farm lanes where the cows had trodden, became a sea of mud and we had to wear our wellies each time we crossed to fetch water. One day, having traversed an even more squelchy track than usual, we stopped at the first field, our hearts missing a beat. It was occupied by a Hereford bull, who stood grazing on the far side.

There was no one in sight to assist us and we debated what to do. No other way led to the farmhouse and we wondered if we could make it across, before he spotted us.

The bull appeared to be taking no notice, so we climbed the fence stealthily. When half-way over the field, he suddenly saw us and began advancing. Petrified, we sprinted the rest of the way, envisaging a charging hulk of four hundred weight, his head held down and we vaulted the gate like hunted deer.

On reaching the dairy, Cyril Luckes appeared, mesmerised by our ashen faces.

"You mean you were afraid of Ferdie?" He let out a roar of laughter, holding his sides. "He's as docile as a lamb!"

Next day, there was a knock on the caravan door. Yvonne opened it to find Cyril Luckes standing there with the bull!

"Meet Ferdie," he said. "Come on, stroke him," and he put his arm round him.

We did. Ferdie moved his head up and down in enjoyment waiting for more!

The spring provided the usual orphan fledglings in their scores and our patients were increasing. All kinds of garden, moorland, woodland and water birds were brought to us by workers on the estate and Brian continued to bring us casualties at the shop. We also found ourselves caring for baby foxes, a squirrel and even a polecat. In time, we erected additional aviaries upon the green.

Alas, not only was the hospital capacity increasing but it was becoming obvious that the rats were, too. On discovering one in an aviary hunting for food one day, we called to Rusty.

"Rat…! Rat!" The very word caused him to go wild with excitement. His hackles stood up, the whites of his eyes gleamed and tearing away at the wire from beneath the ground, he burrowed his way in. The terrified victim had shot up into a tree in the aviary but Rusty shook the tree madly in his paws and pulled that up as well. In an instant, he had seized the rat and tossed it into the air, dead.

That night, as we were lying in bed, high-pitched squeals came from beneath the caravan. They had come to live underneath! Rusty scratched feverishly, whimpering to get out and after we had opened the door, his excited barking echoed each time he caught one. But soon, there were far too many for him to deal with. We had become infested.

The summer passed and the wrath of winter began approaching. The journey for water in the early mornings became cold and miserable. Cyril Luckes, seeing us frozen, would invite us into the farmhouse and call to his wife to provide us with 'a drop of hard stuff', before going on our way. It was welcome and we would warm ourselves in front of the cheerful, log fire.

"Do the children still come and see your hospital?" his wife asked chattily one day.

"Regularly, despite the weather," we told her. "Simon loves making up names for them all. They really are a delightful family."

She agreed and mumbled thoughtfully, "I often think about that terrible gypsy curse upon them and wonder if it's true."

"What curse?"

"Have you never heard? The 1st Earl who bought the estate in the 17th century made a servant girl pregnant and wouldn't marry her. She came from gypsy stock and swore by bell, book and candle that every heir should die young."

"And have they?"

"Yes. Every single one has met an early death if you read about it, although the family doesn't believe the curse." She shrugged. "But you can take it whichever way you like."

We shuddered but time was getting near for us to go into the shop and we were preoccupied by our own worries. There had even been another robbery. We had decided the only thing to do was to part with Rusty and to leave him on guard at night. We shut him in the room where we kept the most valuable items and felt sure that his loud barking and his very presence would be enough to deter any intruder.

But we were wrong. A week later there was another break-in and the police captured a well-known, local jail-bird by the name of Albie Ford. (If Rusty had been let loose, he would virtually have killed him.) But the goods were missing. He had thrown them into the Thames. All that was ever recovered was a canteen of cutlery which appeared for sale at a shop in Reading.

To add to our troubles, that bitterly cold winter had no respite. Water froze and conditions became extreme. After enduring it for as long as we could, we knew we could not undergo another winter in the caravan again.

Some months later, we heard a rumour that a shop with partly furnished living accommodation had become vacant in Oxford Street, at the top end of the town. It was owned by Geoff Thompson, a coal merchant and we raced into Newbury to see him. We begged him to let it to us and he agreed. It was August and time for us to move.

On the day of our departure, as we were dismantling the aviaries, the children came to say goodbye to the patients, with tears in their eyes.

"Please still come and visit us and bring your wildlife to release upon the estate," the whole family begged.

We gave them our promise and did so as often as we could.

CHAPTER 8
1969

As we moved into number 33 Oxford Street which was four-hundred-and-forty years old, we discovered a perfect setting for a White Hall farce. In fact, we found ourselves having fun exploring and wondering what we would find next.

Immediately behind the small shop, we came face to face with a bath. Modernising the premises had meant installing it in the open completely on its own, without a door or curtain. Filling it meant running a hosepipe from a miniature water heater in the kitchen.

Narrow stairs led up to the next floor at an angle of forty-five degrees, so that anyone with any kind of handicap could never have gone up them. At the top we met with a loo, again without a door and in full view. Maybe the designer had lived in the Australian Bush.

On the right, a bedroom contained just a double bed, on the left was a boxroom, while another set of stairs led to two rooms in the attic.

It was the sort of place which one would expect to possess a ghost or even secret panels and while I was messing about, feeling around the staircase walls, a panel gave way and slid to the side! We waited with bated breath. It contained nothing at all.

We settled all our patients in their new home in the small garden to the rear, while Rusty and Eno sniffed around the cramped spaces. There was no room for intensive care patients, so we put an injured barn owl, which characteristically wanted to hide itself away, into the dark cupboard under the stairs.

Once we had erected our board, 'The Newbury Wildlife Hospital', over the door of the shop, feeling dead beat, we slumped on to the double bed. We got no sleep at all. Springs stuck out at all angles and in the morning, I said, "I've had enough of that. That's going out of the window." It did forthwith—in the direction by which it had come in fifty years ago!

However, the brass plate on the premises next door suggested some good news. The engraving advertised a vet's named 'Addis & Warde' and we soon had need for them. The public did not take long to become aware of our new abode and the voice of a policeman on the telephone in the middle of the night, reported an injured badger. We got into the van and journeyed six miles in the darkness along the Hungerford road, where the police car was waiting with flashing lights. At the side of the road lay the poor creature, an adult dog badger, quite defenceless and which made no resistance to being picked up and brought home.

We rang the vet's number and Mr. John Addis appeared straight from his bed, his hair tousled. On seeing what we'd brought, his eyes popped out of his head.

"Badgers are vicious!" he hissed, as if it were a lion.

I laid it on the table.

"You'd better hold it," he stated, as if about to be attacked and while I did so with an amused expression, he sedated it before he dared examine it!

Badger required some stitches to his front and we brought him back asleep, to recover.

Next day we spent attempting to make the living

accommodation more habitable, by laying pieces of carpet and erecting a few shelves. I busied myself, hammering away while Yvonne waited poised with the nails.

A day later the smell of gas began invading the building. Yvonne searched the cooker for leaking taps but there was no sign of any. Yet the smell got worse. By four o'clock we were coughing and wearing yashmaks and felt compelled to ring the Gas Board.

The fellow arrived in record time and he puffed away with his 'squeegee' bottle along the pipes. Suddenly, flinging open the cupboard where Barny was, he announced, "It's in here!"

We made a grab for Barny, horrified that he may have been gassed. But after investigation, the man decided he was wrong. He then began pulling up the carpet and floorboards. "No, it's here!" he called, triumphantly. "Someone's put a nail through the gas pipe." It was the very last place one would have expected to have found one!

Inspector Brian called in next day with an injured rabbit and in his cheerful way, stopped to help us reinforce a cage for Badger. Badger was beginning to recover and we knew he would need a good, strong cage with an aluminium floor. Badgers are extremely strong animals and we had learned from experience that they can dig their way out. Within an hour, Brian had finished the job and without even stopping for a cup of tea, dashed off to a meeting.

Our next task was to make order out of chaos in our ransacked antique shop at West Mills. We had given notice to the landlord and there were a few valueless items of bric-a-brac plus a broken chamber pot to be collected, which the burglars had not wanted. Also, luckily a few pieces of our own furniture remained and surprise, surprise!—amongst them were my musical instruments, still wrapped up. We brought everything back.

How good it was to strum on them once again! That evening we amused ourselves by singing the good old songs from our night-club days. Eno sat with his ears cocked up while Rusty joined in, with loud howls.

During those carefree hours, little did we know what life held in store for us the next morning.

We were greeted by the voice of Brian on the telephone. "Could I bring you some swans in a terrible state?" He went on to explain that a tanker had tipped a large quantity of oil into one of the gravel pits that had formed a lake at Thatcham.

He arrived in no time with the poor creatures in his van. As he opened the door, the sight made us gasp in horror. There were as many as thirteen, the upper halves of their bodies, their heads and wings a mass of thick, black grease.

We knew time was not on our side and hoped that they had not swallowed too much oil in trying to preen themselves, which is the killer. Using a funnel and a lengthy tube in the way that we had done for Archie, the heron, we inserted vitamins from John Addis down each of their throats, to replace their body fluids.

Now came the problem of cleaning their plumage. Yvonne could remember seeing some old-fashioned tin baths in Hitchman's, the builders' yard opposite and popped over to ask if we could borrow them. They agreed and we brought them home. The hard work was about to begin. Rubbing Swarfega into their plumage like two people gone crazy, we then immersed each bird in a bath of hot water and washing-up liquid, repeating the procedure time and time again. But after hours of sweated labour, all we managed to save were one mother and her cygnet. The rest died in our arms.

The summer was disappearing, the days gradually growing

colder and winter began to make its presence felt again. Then when December neared, we were greeted with sadder news. One morning we heard Brian's van draw up outside the shop and wondered what he had come to tell us.

"I've just heard that I've been offered the job of Regional Organiser in Hexham, Northumberland."

It was a shock. Brian had come to Newbury fresh out of college and we realised that one day, he would have to apply for promotion but we had never expected him to go so far away.

"When do you begin?" we asked.

"The 1st January."

"I shall be very sorry to be leaving here, though," he added. "It's been a great time."

We were equally as sorry. His cheery countenance and ever helping-hand had become second-nature and he would be sadly missed.

"You can't keep a good man down," Yvonne said bravely, forcing a smile.

"Where's that bottle of Champagne that we had at Church House?" I asked when I had recovered, "the one left over from the day the Festival Queen came?"

I found it, opened it with a loud 'pop', then poured three glasses.

"Here's to the future and here's to the past," I said. "You deserve it, Brian. Congratulations!" and raising ours, we drank to his new post.

CHAPTER 9
1970

When the warmth of spring returned, every day Rusty stretched himself out in a disinterested fashion in the open shop doorway. One morning, however, he sat bolt upright as a man appeared bearing a box with distinct scuffling coming from it. We opened it up and Rusty sniffed inside. Four baby fox-cubs were huddled together, their mother having been shot by a gamekeeper.

The tiny, helpless things were still blind and we took them from him, settling them in a weaning box filled with straw in the boxroom. They were like shapeless, brown, woolly puppies with pug faces and it was a joy to hold them, as they suckled a baby's bottle of lacto, the mother substitute, every two hours. Amongst them were two dog foxes and we named them Tom and Jerry.

Rusty meanwhile, continued to spend his days lying dejectedly in the shop doorway, obviously missing his rat-chasing and open fields.

But the fox-cubs thrived in their new home. Their eyes opened at ten days and soon we weaned them on to tinned cat or dog meat, watching their little bodies beginning to take shape and their legs growing. By the time they were six weeks old, their coats had turned red and they adopted the look of foxes with pointed faces, the lower-half white. They were like mischievous puppies, spending their time romping and squealing and we put them in the shop window, much to the delight of the passers-by.

The fox-cubs were happy but Rusty was not. Suddenly we

noticed with concern that he was starting to become aggressive to people, daring anyone to enter the shop and when we rebuked him, each time he lay down growling and sullen, his head on his paws.

The days passed and the problem got no better.

"Do you think we ought to find a new home for him?" I often suggested in despair. Suddenly there was a commotion in the street and a man came rushing in shouting, "Your dog grabbed me by the trouser leg and pulled me over." We knew we must do something urgently. That week we advertised in the newspaper and a reply came from a retired policeman. He had been a dog-handler and was eager for a pet of his own. We explained the situation to him and he said he would like to come and see us. When he arrived, instead of snarling at him, Rusty regarded him passively with his usual intelligent, brown eyes. The man was obviously one whom animals respected. He talked to Rusty in gentle tones and told us he had an adequate garden and a large exercise ground nearby, where he felt he could make a happy animal of him again. We agreed to let him have Rusty for a trial period.

It was with great sadness that we said goodbye to our dear Rusty and his new master promised to give a weekly report.

Despite the busy street in which we lived, we noticed there were several owls living in the trees of a large house to the rear. Most people think of owls as rural birds but many a story is told of the well-known Tawny inhabiting populated areas and adapting to humans.

One evening as soon as it became dark, I stood at the upstairs back window giving a quavering 'Woo woo' and held out a piece of meat in my hand. Within two to three minutes, an owl swooped down and took it! I scarcely felt a thing. All I knew was that the titbit had gone. The next night I tried it again and the same thing happened. Soon, the entire owl population got to know.

One day, the owner of the house brought one to us that she had found lying in her garden. We discovered that he was suffering from fits. His little body would go into sudden contortions and we treated him by dousing him in water. After the fit was over, he would appear quite normal again. We let him live indoors and he became a regular member of the household. When we went into the hotel nearby, we would take him with us and the staff there got to know him and gave him lettuce.

Our faithful old van had given up the ghost and we had been forced to trade it in for a cheap, second-hand, estate car. Tawny came with us to buy it, possessing the cheek of the devil. As soon as the door was opened, he flew in and perched himself on the steering-wheel. After being relegated to the back, he sat at the rear window looking out. Motorists behind thought he was a stuffed owl until he gave a sudden spring from one side to the other, surprising the daylights out of them. Yvonne spent her time amusing herself looking out of the window, watching their faces.

The retired constable who had taken Rusty was as good as his word and gave us regular news of him. He was settling down well in his new home and now with plenty of exercise, had become a contented, docile dog again. We went over to visit him and he bounded upon us like long, lost souls. Upon seeing Eno, the two began romping around in their usual fashion, Eno putting his head in Rusty's mouth. Rusty was happy but had obviously missed us as much as we had missed him and when we returned home, we could only console ourselves by occupying our minds with other things.

Now instead of Rusty, it was Tawny who had taken over the shop and with the licence of a court jester. His favourite position was perched upon the top of the door, staring at customers as they came in and totally ignoring them. In fact, it was so commonplace to see him up there that we would go about our every-day business, forgetting all about him. But one day he gave us a more than gentle reminder of his presence.

A man entered carrying a swift, cupped in his hands. Yvonne waited ready to take it from him, when suddenly a louse hopped out from under the bird's wing. It was the species which commonly inhabits swifts—an ugly-looking insect like a miniature green crab. The man gave a loud, "Ugh!" and let the swift go. In a trice, Tawny zoomed down and had it. His talons penetrated so deeply into the poor creature that there was no way in which we could save it.

Mid-August arrived and the once baby foxes were now reaching adulthood, healthy, romping and snarling in their play. Although reared in captivity, we began to realise that they were developing the instincts of the wild. They were three months old now and were becoming cautious and even savage, making it necessary to handle them with gloves on. Strangely enough, they never once hurt Yvonne. Yvonne possessed a certain way with animals—some kind of affinity—which they responded to. I can even remember her once feeding dingoes in a zoo!

It was without doubt, time to let them go and we decided to telephone the keeper of a wildlife park that had opened up at Weyhill, near Andover. He said he would be interested in taking them and we drove them there in the car, where we were met by him. As we opened the door to take them out, he insisted, "I'll do it"—and before we could stop him, Tom had given him a hefty bite on the hand!

It was six months later that we happened to revisit the park and couldn't believe our eyes. Tom and Jerry had grown so large that they were pacing up and down as if they were wolves!

Yet now, it was still August and something quite unusual occurred. A brochure was dropped through everyone's door announcing that we were going to have a local radio station. It would be called Radio Oxford, would be opening on the 18th October and they wanted to hear from the public with any items of local news and features of interest.

"Well, what about our hospital?" we thought and decided to telephone them. They were very interested and in surprisingly quick time, sent their van to record us in situ.

The team spent some time deciding where they wanted to rig up their equipment and what they wanted to feature, then at last their outside broadcaster commenced the interview, chatting as he went round the hospital.

"When will we be on?" we asked when it was all over.

"On Friday the 25th October, at eleven o'clock," we were told. It was all very exciting.

That morning Yvonne switched on in anticipation and tuned into Medium Wave, 95.0 megahertz. "Here we are! Listen!"

"Now we are going to Newbury to somewhere quite unique. At number 33 Oxford Street, live two ladies who run a Wildlife Hospital out of their own money. Here we are at their shop and they even have two kestrels perched in the window!"

"Good morning. I'm Pete from Radio Oxford. You must be Louise and Yvonne Veness. And who is this lovely, silky-black Pekinese in Yvonne's arms?"

Yvonne: "This is Eno."

Eno: 'Woof, woof!'

Pete: "Hallo, Eno. I'm being licked. Thank you, I've had a wash today. Are you coming with us round the Wildlife Hospital, too? I can't wait to see it."

Louise: "Come on, then. Let's go through to the garden."

Pete: "Well, here we are in the garden. It's only small, but what a host of cages of every size is packed into it and all filled with patients. I can see owls, a magpie, a squirrel, a cock pheasant with a stumpy foot… Do you call him Peg Leg…? And what have we here, a pair of 'peewits' (or lapwings)?"

Louise: "Yes, they're my favourite birds, because they're never aggressive. They are always so gentle—and yet I always call them little military birds because of the way they march up and down in their smart black and white uniform, with a crest in their beret. But we've discovered with peewits that if you are not prepared to find mealworms or maggots for them, so that they can peck or forage for their insects on the ground, they will die."

Pete: "But oh my, what is this in the next cage? A beautiful, little, red-brown animal with cream underparts.

And what a smart black tip to his tail!"

Yvonne: "That's Stanley the stoat, growing his thick winter coat. But if he lived in the north, he'd change to a pure white so that he could be camouflaged in the snow. Nature is wonderful, isn't it? But he'd still keep his black tip to his tail."

Pete: "Would he be called an ermine then?"

Yvonne: "Yes—and with just one black tip to every ermine, think how many of those poor little creatures must have been caught to make the fur on the coronation robes."

Pete: "Or on Father Christmas's cloak. Is he vicious?"

Louise: "Yes. Don't put your finger through his cage. You would need a pair of spiky gloves."

Pete: "And what a variety of waterlife you have, too! A swan, a moorhen with only one wing, a seagull and several cheeky ducks coming up to me and quacking for food.

Have you any for them?"

Yvonne: "Here, throw them these peanuts."

Pete: "Peanuts? Do they like those? Oh yes! Now, now, stop it, you greedy lot! They're scrabbling all over my feet."

Yvonne: "You'd be surprised how many birds and animals like peanuts."

Louise: "If we take you indoors, we have another hospital ward to show you, in the boxroom."

Pete: "Right, off we go. We're climbing up the stairs now and here's the door. Well, look what's in here! A female badger, sound asleep in a box of straw."

Louise: "She was the victim of badger baiting. There were two others and they died. It's a terrible thing. But at least she has no young at this time of the year."

Pete: "What do you call her?"

Yvonne: "Bella."

Pete: "We'll leave her in peace and go downstairs quietly.

Hey, what on earth? It scared the living daylights out of me!

A flying object from outer space has landed on Louise's shoulder. It's an owl."

We laughed and laughed.

Louise: "That's Tawny. So, you've been hiding, you naughty boy!"

We told him how Tawny lived indoors and sat on top of the shop door.

Pete: "Well, that's remarkable. Thank you so much for showing me round. These two ladies are certainly doing a worthwhile job. Before I leave, what record would you like me to play?"

We told him and the sounds of the orchestra rang forth on the air. Our choice simply had to be 'The Thieving Magpie'.

CHAPTER 10
1971

A year had passed since our antique shop had opened, but trade was poor. Radio Oxford had brought us more interest but it was obvious that we needed more significant premises and we asked the owner for permission to enlarge the window. He shook his head.

"It's a listed building, I'm afraid and in no way can its structure be altered."

However, when the springtime came, there was better news. We learned that number 31, the adjoining shop, which had a far better window was to become vacant. We had an idea and contacted Mr. Thompson again. We asked if we might move next door and sub-let number 33, which would give us two gardens for our wildlife.

He agreed. We soon found a tenant for number 33 and friends helped us to move in next door. Now that we possessed an extra garden, we decided to make a much-needed pond. We worked a whole weekend at it and after we had finished, we introduced our patients to their new habitat. They appeared to be enjoying themselves and it was fun watching them dabbling and dive-bombing for the bread and peanuts that we threw to them.

As soon as we had settled in, Tawny took up his position like a sentry over this shop door, every bit as impudent as before. He even treated the house as if he owned it. If we left the bedroom door open, we would find him in there. But one morning, when we returned from shopping in the town, he was nowhere to be seen.

"Tawny!" we called. "TAWN-EE!" again and again but there was no response.

We hunted everywhere on the ground floor but no pair of eyes blinked at us from a height and no flying object swooped down on to my shoulder. We felt worried and searched the first floor with still no luck. As a last resort, we climbed up to the attic. There he was—on the floor, pulling up the corner of the heavy carpet which we could scarcely lift ourselves, having a game with it!

As time went on, trade began to pick up. Items of bric-a-brac slowly drifted in, even porcelain and clocks, and customers were taking an interest.

All at once, this shop began to have its amusing experiences, as at West Mills. Some youngsters entered one Saturday lugging four musical instrument cases between them. They stood them down, to reveal inside the largest a base trombone. Next, they opened the other three and out came a trumpet, a cornet and a French horn. "Right, we'll try and sell them for you," we said and put them in the window.

On the Sunday morning there was a knock on the door and it was a police sergeant. "I'm sorry to say that the instruments in your window have been stolen from The Salvation Army."

A month or so later another young lad came in. "My grandmother has died and left me these. Would you buy them? I need the money."

He delved into a bag and out came two superb bronze figures of horses, two bronze vases and a candelabrum, which he arranged on the counter. Not knowing their value, we gave him £20, worth far more in those days than today.

It was lucky for the Queen that we did not sell them. Before we could do so, we received another visit from the police sergeant making enquiries in the area, to inform us that they had been lifted from the Racecourse, from the Royal Box!

The summer passed and brought the usual abandoned baby swifts, housemartins and swallows—offsprings of late broods, left behind by their parents. Some developed in time to follow across the multitudinous seas and the rest, unlikely to survive, faced the unnaturalness of a winter world.

Christmas came round again before we had scarcely realised it and two friends of ours invited us to have a drink with them in 'The Cooper's Arms'. As we sat around a table, warming ourselves with a tot of Whisky, they introduced us to the landlords, John and Vicky Cunnington.

"This place needs livening up, doesn't it?" our friends commented after a while.

"I've got an electric organ," I remarked as a joke.

To my surprise, John had overheard and exclaimed, "What a good idea! Could you play it for us?"

"If you really want me to," I replied, "I'll bring it along."

The next night we brought the organ and a microphone with us and "I'm Dreaming of a White Christmas" began to flow from it, accompanied by Yvonne in her sweet, soprano voice. The walls vibrated and that old pub sprang to life once again. When it was over, the customers who had gathered around listening gave a loud cheer and requests came for different numbers from all round.

"Do you think you could play for us every weekend?" John asked. "We will pay you."

"Certainly!" we agreed.

And so it came about that John and Vicky hung a poster in

their window stating: -

Come here and listen to
Musical Entertainment
upon the Electric Organ
by
THE VIBRANT VENICES
Every Friday, Saturday & Sunday Night.
You'll be sure to enjoy yourselves!

The job was heaven-sent. The extra money was just what we needed to keep our wildlife.

CHAPTER 11
1972

On New Year's Eve, much frivolity reigned in The Cooper's Arms. As soon as Big Ben struck the twelve notes of midnight, John crossed the threshold bearing a lump of coal and wished everyone 'A Happy New Year'. Then all joined in a circle singing Auld Lang Syne and when "Time gentlemen, please," had to be called to the regret of all, Yvonne led the customers in a chain out into the street dancing the Conga. A police car was patrolling the area and they stopped the car and kissed the policeman!

We returned home at last on that icy cold night, to snatch the few hours' sleep that remained.

When the spring came, we had a nice, little fellow brought to us, a baby magpie, scarcely having left the nest and we named him Magnus. We hand-reared him on maggots, egg, grain and fruit and as he grew, we marvelled at his black pantaloons and smart, white waistcoat. He was a perky, little chap and amused himself, springing around his cage or playing for hours bathing in his bowl of drinking water, tipping it up in the process. As he matured, his tail formed with its green sheen and his colouring became even more outstanding.

One weekend the shop door opened and in came a lady holding a thrush. She explained that she had discovered it sitting beneath a tree in her garden, obviously unwell.

I took it from her and noticed a tick attached to its forehead, right above its eye. I pulled it off as one does from a dog or cat's fur and to my chagrin, the poor little creature died instantly. The parasite must have been adhering to its brain.

"What a host of horrible things there are in this world, aren't there?" I exclaimed. "It reminds me of the greenbottle fly which lays her eggs in the nose of the toad. The larvae live on that animal's brain and slowly kill it in the same way. Quite revolting!" I added with a shudder.

"Well, that poor little thrush has brought me to your antique shop," she remarked, as if noticing it for the first time and her eyes wandered to a deep blue teapot on the shelf, which had a frieze of white, Grecian figures.

I took it down. "It's an Adams, dated about 1860. Adams amalgamated with Wedgwood, you know."

"It's beautiful. It's my aunt's seventieth birthday next week. How much is it?"

"It has a slight chip on the rim, so I'll say £6."

"I'll take it."

She handed me a £10 note and while I was searching for the change, I heard Yvonne calling, "Eno, come on! Come on in!"

It wasn't his meal time and I hoped he wasn't chasing the ducks.

The lady departed and I went out into the garden. Yvonne was nowhere in sight and Eno was sitting quite inoffensively under the shrubs.

I went into the kitchen. "Why did you call Eno?"

"I didn't."

"I'm sure I heard you."

"No, I've been here all the time. You've gone doolally."

Suddenly, from the garden there came a laugh. It was an exact copy of Yvonne's and we both went out to the direction from which it had come. Two wicked black eyes were staring at us from a cage.

"Magnus! You're the culprit, you cheeky rascal!" Yvonne cried.

She went over to him, opened his cage and let him perch on her finger. "You're growing up!"

As if showing off again, Magnus took off and alighted on a bush two feet away, proving that he could fly.

"Good boy!" we applauded.

"Can't he acclimatise in the garden now?" I suggested. (We always scattered pieces of bacon fat and corn on the ground for visiting birds and there was plenty of food around the pond. He could fly away whenever he was ready.)

"Yes, he looks contented enough there," Yvonne agreed. "We'll leave him."

From that day on, Magnus spent his time happily springing around the garden or watching the world from his favourite elder tree, with no wish to go.

One day in the summer we received a surprise. Mr. Thompson, our landlord, called to see us. He informed us that he had received a request from the D.H.S.S. who were desperate to find accommodation for one of their employees who was coming from Newcastle. Number 33 next door was vacant once again and Mr. Thompson had agreed that Mr. Garside and his wife could take up possession at the beginning of July. But we were concerned about our wildlife. Where could they be housed?

"No need to worry. You can still keep the garden," he replied kindly, "but when the Garsides arrive, will you let them have the key?"

Nevertheless, we *were* worried. What if the Garsides were not an amenable couple and were opposed to the hospital in their backyard? We waited until July with trepidation.

Upon the first, the large removal van from Northumberland drew up outside the door, followed by the Garsides in their car. They came round immediately for the key. They were a middle-aged couple and it was amusing to see their faces as Tawny swooped down on to my shoulder and Eno bombarded them for fuss.

"We'll bring you round a cup of tea," we said.

"Thank you. That is kind. We're tired out. We've been on the road since six and we're suffering from removal lag."

When the van had gone, they came round to return the tray and introduced themselves as May and Jim.

We told them our friend, Brian Sanders, the RSPCA Inspector, had been promoted to Northumberland. "Best Inspector we've ever known," we said. "We still miss him."

"Where did he go to?" Jim replied.

"Hexham."

"Oh yes, we know it well."

"Do tell us all about your wildlife," May asked. "Maybe we could feed them for you any time you need a break?"

After half-an-hour, it became obvious that our fears about uncooperative neighbours were quite groundless.

Next morning, the telephone rang and it was the police. "There's a swan in the middle of the road holding up the traffic at Wash Common. Please could you come?"

Wash Common is south-west of Newbury on the busy main A343 Andover Road. We said we would come straight away and started up the 'ambulance'. When we arrived at the scene ten minutes later, there was the policeman standing watching the swan, too scared to touch it!

After a while I succeeded in luring it again into a garden, then making a grab for the back of its neck in the usual way and practicing the 'swan-hold', I brought it back to the car and put it on Yvonne's lap. Then, much to the amusement of all, we drove off with it and put it on the river.

When we arrived back home again, we were greeted by May Garside calling from next door. "I went outside to put something in the dustbin and was scared out of my wits. A voice behind me suddenly called, 'Eno, come in. Come on in!' Then I spotted it. What do you think it was? A magpie on the windowsill!"

***

The number of customers at 'The Cooper's Arms' was increasing, much to the delight of John and Vicky Cunnington, who offered to buy us a present of a second microphone, as one was becoming inadequate. This meant a trip to Reading and one day we set out on the seventeen-mile journey to 'The Butts Centre' music shop.

I was immediately in my element, looking at the array of musical instruments ranging from guitars to grand pianos. Before going on stage, I had owned a music shop and now I became immersed again in the days when I had even held talent competitions. It was then that I had discovered the young lad called Percy Swinscoe, the Ventriloquist, who was destined to become a member of The Black and White Minstrel Show. Percy had joined me in the trio with Neville King before Yvonne and I formed 'The Venices'.

"Just look at this!" I heard Yvonne calling suddenly from the other end of the shop. She had found a double keyboard, the latest design, a Magnetta and I went to see it.

"Don't tempt me!" I replied, eyeing it enviously.

"Can I help you, Madam?" asked a voice behind us. It was

the Manager with the scent of business in his nostrils.

"No thank you," I replied definitely. "I could never afford that!"

"It has a beautiful tone," he insisted, "and all the latest attachments. Why not play it?" and indicated the chair. "It'll cost you nothing to try it."

"I'll try it," I laughed, "but that will be all."

I sat down and my fingers ran along the keys, playing 'Moon River'. The tone was superb.

"I could allow you a twenty per cent discount on it," he coaxed, determined not to be outdone.

My mouth watered but nevertheless I stood up, refusing again, paid for the microphone and left the shop.

"Let's have a cup of tea before going back," I suggested and we went into a nearby café. As we were sipping our tea, Yvonne remarked, "You really would love that keyboard, wouldn't you?"

"Our wildlife is more important," I asserted. "Our opulent days are gone."

"That chap really wants business, doesn't he?" she replied. "Could we go back again? I have an idea."

"*You* can, if you like."

Off she went and I remained behind.

"Would it be possible to pay for it monthly?" she asked. "That's the only way we could ever afford it."

To my amazement, she returned clutching the keyboard.

"However, did you get that?" I asked.

"The Manager agreed to let me have it on H.P. I paid the first instalment and here we are!"

It had been a happy day and we arrived home in time to give the afternoon feed. Soon we had the pans of bread ready, lettuce for the waterfowl, chopped stewing steak, peanuts, fish and grated cheese and went into the garden.

But how swiftly life can become transformed into sadness. As we reached the pond, we looked in dismay. Floating on the surface was the pathetic little body of Magnus. His love of water had caused his death. He had been unable to get out of the pond and had drowned. Too late, we realised that the pond was not stepped.

We rescued him with tears in our eyes and prepared to bury him, contemplating where it should be. It didn't take long. We laid him to rest beneath his favourite elder tree.

CHAPTER 12
1973

The month of March arrived and there came a surprise. The telephone rang and at the other end was the voice of a farmer from Watership Down. "I have an injured short-eared owl in my barn. Please could you come and collect it?"

The prospect was exciting. We had never had such an owl at the hospital. Short-eared owls are inhabitants of the north and Scotland and only occasionally come south, in the autumn and winter months.

We got out the 'ambulance', travelled on the Basingstoke road and turned off to Ecchinswell. Watership Down was the scene of Richard Adams' later famous novel and having passed through the village, we climbed uphill and downhill, uphill and downhill successively until we were right out in the wilds. There was not a soul in sight but a lone stroller.

"Do you happen to know where Ashley Warren Farm is?" we called.

"Nope, I don't."

We climbed up another hill and down again, with still no sign of the farm. Eventually, an old country yokel approached on a bike.

"We're looking for Ashley Warren Farm. Do you know it?"

He pulled up. "Yer find it down yonder." He indicated a narrow road to the right.

We took that direction. The road continued for what seemed

miles into no-mans-land, with fields and open land on either side.

"Do you think there really is a farm?" I remarked.

"Well, we're coming to a track. I suppose that leads somewhere."

We bumped along it for what seemed even more miles.

"Do you think we're still in England?"

"I doubt it."

After a while Yvonne cried, "Look, there's something in the distance. They must be farm buildings, surely?"

She was right. As we neared them it became obvious that the farmhouse was to the fore and a bit further on, a gate appeared with a sign on it: 'Ashley Warren Farm'.

As Yvonne climbed out to undo the gate, the farmer's wife spotted us and came out, leading us to the barn where the patient was ready in a box.

It was worth the journey, to find 'Pussy'. It was a female and her wide eyes were yellow like a cat's with vertical slits. We discovered she had a broken wing and we took her home, mended it and put her to rest in confinement.

Short-eared owls have a special spot in Yvonne's affections because of their attractive expressions. Their eyes are unlike other owls which have no slits and their 'ears' are not ears at all, but simply tufts of feathers. Another unusual characteristic of short-eared owls is that they can be seen hunting by day, with their curious flapping flight, searching for their main diet of voles. One owl can eat as many as sixteen a day!

But the sad thing was, we had none to feed her with. Of course, we had the usual chopped beef for her but we knew Pussy was longing for her voles. Then we had an idea. We would ask the public and put her in her cage in the window with a notice:

PLEASE COULD YOU HELP?

*I LOVE VOLES AND MICE AND HAVE NONE TO EAT.
IF YOUR CATS CATCH ANY, PLEASE COULD YOU
BRING THEM FOR ME?*

It worked. One lady who possessed several cats, brought us a bagful of little victims. She told us proudly that she had stored them all up in her deep-freeze!

Next came Kee-kee, the kestrel. We often had hawks as patients and I always made sure to handle them with strong gloves. I had learned to my cost that their hooked talons can penetrate the human skin and are unreleasable.

Kestrels hover and swoop for their prey at the verges of motorways and Kee-kee had flown into the side of a car. Now, he was a sad spectacle with his tail missing. After a period of rest, his former self reappeared but he had lost his ability to fly.

In another cage we had had Kerry, a female kestrel, who had also had an accident but had not survived. Only that morning I had found her dead and the sad task of burying her had yet to be done. I looked at her beautiful, fan-shaped tail and wished it were Kee-kee's. Then I stopped. Would it be possible to give it to Kee-kee—a sort of transplant? I pulled out first one feather, then another, until I had at least a dozen. Then agog with the idea, I fetched the Superglue.

"Hold Kee-kee for me, will you?" I instructed Yvonne, then gluing one, inserted it firmly into a quill, then the next and continued until he had a complete tail. Kee-kee accepted it without demurring but the question was, would it work? Maybe he would need time to adjust to it mentally and we disappeared indoors, to take care of the shop.

It wasn't until the evening, as I was locking up, that Yvonne called to me as she was coming in from the garden. "Guess what I've just seen? Kee-kee has flown off his perch!"

I went out there. He was looking at me cheekily, his rufous back contrasting with his yellow breast and his black eyes fierce. With his female tail, he looked a startling new bird—and as if to show off, he retrieved a piece of meat and flew back on to his perch to eat it.

It seemed as if he would be able to be released, so in the morning I lifted him out and we watched him fly exultantly over the rooftops to his freedom.

A week passed by and as usual, I arose at six o'clock to prepare the morning feed and begin the duty round of the hospital. Once out in the garden, I stopped in my tracks.

"Look who's here!" I called to Yvonne. It was always our policy to leave the cage door open once a bird had gone and sitting back in his cage was Kee-kee!

Yvonne came out right away. "Oh dear, oh dear! Was that big, wide world outside too terrible for you?" and added, "He prefers his two Aunties at the hospital."

"He's absolutely ravenous!" I asserted. "Here, give him his breakfast—beef and chicken."

He took it, then quietly we shut his door and went on our way.

With the spring came the usual influx of nestlings and fledglings, amongst which was a nest of wagtails, together with tits and finches and a man brought us yet another owl—but not a short-eared. It was a run-of-the-mill, baby Tawny, which he had found in the woods at Bucklebury when walking his dog. We hand-reared him and as we knew owls are not mature until they are four months old, Hector had board and lodgings with us until the early autumn.

In the summer, everywhere in the arable fields the detestable crop-spraying began and the substance was carried by the wind in all directions, reaching not only the farmers' young calves themselves but a nest of sparrowhawks, high in a tree. Two of the young were brought to us.

Diarrhoea is a sure sign of poisoning. Their feathers were dropping out and in every such case, we administer Johnson's Avon Mixture as a first aid measure, in the hope of clearing it from their bodies. As chance would have it, these survived but they were paralysed and never able to fly. To show the public what tragedies can occur through man's lack of thought, we put them in the window for all to witness.

Soon the summer drew to an end, when the annual migration began taking place. In no time, the great exodus was in full swing but at the same time, an equally great ingress of birds was arriving from the Arctic or over the North Sea to spend the winter with us. How marvellous a thing is nature and the great world around us!

October was here and it was time to release Hector, now a healthy juvenile and as we were aware of where he was born, we decided to return him to his original home when it was dusk. That evening, we set out on the minor B4009 north-east of Newbury. Approximately five miles further on, we drove over the bridge of the dismantled railway line, turned right past Fisher's Farm and on to Bucklebury Alley—a lane full of large houses—which led to the woods.

Darkness had fallen when we drew up, took the cage from the 'ambulance' and walked through the trees. As we opened the door of the cage, Hector flew away with only a moment's hesitation into dense foliage and there was silence. We waited quietly for ten minutes for any sound of him, calling him at the same time but there was no response. At last, feeling fairly satisfied that he must be acclimatising to his old surroundings, we walked back to the road.

As I started up the car, we spotted a yellow flashing light rotating in the distance. I began to move out to the right, thinking it was a police car or an ambulance—but as I approached to circumnavigate it, the object took off into the air and swiftly and silently, disappeared into the night.

I drove to the spot where it had ascended and stopped, unable to go any further. There were trees blocking the path. There were no turnings off and no hills to give the impression that it was going up—so what on earth was it that we had seen? We had both witnessed it and knew we were not dreaming. It could only have been a U.F.O.

Next day, we telephoned The Department of the Environment at Bristol.

"U.F.O.s *have* been sighted in the area," replied the voice at the other end of the line. "Did you get a photo of it?"

"Hardly!"

"Then I'm afraid there is no way that it can be recorded. We must have a photo."

To this day, we are still left wondering what it was. Not only are there wondrous things on our earth but in the great space beyond.

CHAPTER 13
1974

"Once the New Year's over, there's always such a lull, isn't there?" complained the customers sitting around the bar at 'The Cooper's Arms'. "Nothing to look forward to. Just ice and snow."

Certainly, the weather outside was cold and menacing.

"Only for us Sassenachs," John replied. "In Scotland they celebrate Burn's Night on the 25th January."

"And what do they get up to then?"

He shrugged. "Pipe in the haggis... drink Whisky... dance drunken reels."

"Anybody any bagpipes?" asked some joker in our direction.

"No bagpipes," I replied, "but I could supply a few Burn's songs."

"I've got a whole book of them if you'd like to borrow it," offered a lady. She was small, mousy haired and called Elsie Hillier.

"Good. Bring it along," I agreed.

She did so and indicated her favourites by singing a few lines of each.

"You've got a good voice, Elsie!" remarked Yvonne. "Have you sung professionally?"

"Well, yes," she replied modestly. "I used to. That's how I met Reg. He played the trumpet and the cornet."

"And the drums," her husband volunteered with a smile.

"Have you still got them?" asked John, who was listening.

"Then why don't we have a party on the 25th? Could you bring them and join Louise and Yvonne?"

"An excellent idea," we said. "The more the merrier."

And so they did. When Burn's Night arrived, anyone who could commandeer a kilt, wore it and the music struck up. Out rang, 'When a laddie meets a lassie comin thro' the Rye' and 'Oh, whistle and I'll come to y' me lad', to name a few and everyone's feet started tapping.

After Reg had made his solo debut on the trumpet with 'Ye banks and braes o' bonnie Doon' with Elsie accompanying him, the applause brought the house down.

As soon as the interval was over, the dance tunes began again. Out rang 'Marie's Wedding' and 'The Gay Gordons', and soon everyone rose to their feet, dragging their partners on to the floor, ending with cheering and calls of, "Encore".

It was with regret when the evening drew to a close but we could say with satisfaction, that a good time had been had by all.

That was the story of how Elsie and Reg came to join us permanently, making it necessary for even another trip to Reading to purchase two more microphones, a large and a small.

In fact, in a month's time, yet another newcomer asked if he could join us, a young man playing 'Country and Western' on his guitar and very successful at attracting the youth to the pub. No longer were we just the two 'Vibrant Venices'. We were a full band.

Our days were as busy as our nights. Shortly afterwards, Henry was brought to join our other patients at the hospital, a poor dejected heron. Herons are very prone to accident with their long legs and Henry's was badly injured. It was a job for a vet and John Addis examined it thoroughly.

"It's broken in more than one place," he affirmed. "I shall

need to plaster it."

While I held the poor, frightened creature firmly in my arm and his beak with my other hand, John applied the white, sticky paste and waited for it to set. Then we brought Henry home to rest. But once in the garden, he began clumping around on it in such an ungainly fashion, making us laugh, that the cheery little Newbury Weekly News photographer, who was called Ron Lambert, came and took a 12" x 9" photo of him and myself and it appeared with the caption 'Henry is plastered'—a good advert for us and the vet as well!

May and Jim next door were highly amused by Henry, often bringing him treats of herrings. In fact, May came regularly to see the patients when she had a free moment, repeating that she would take care of the hospital for us any time we wanted a breather. It was April and we thought about it. Now was the time to take advantage of out-of-season rates, wasn't it? Yes, we would take her offer up and have a week's camping holiday in Devon.

Of course, Tawny would have to come with us in the car, plus any intensive care patients. To leave Tawny behind would be unthinkable and Eno would be absolutely lost without him.

On Saturday 13th, we said, "Goodbye," to May and Jim and set out on the one-hundred-and-fifty mile journey to the West Country. At last, we arrived at our camping site at Brixham and although breezy in April, it was truly 'glorious Devon'. As soon as we had erected our tent, we took a packed lunch into the woods nearby and sat watching the stream running through it. To our amusement, Tawny decided to take a bath in it.

Then something happened. Along came a fully-grown badger for a drink. We 'froze', watching in excitement. Then before we could stop him, to our horror Eno ran up to him. But the badger simply sniffed at him and went away!

In the evening, we drove along the coast with its rocky, red cliffs, exploring the beautiful villages and when we came across a village pub which looked inviting, called 'The Ship Inn' at Axmouth, we went in for a drink. As we sat quietly at the bar, we were amused to hear the customers coming in calling, "Look, there's a live owl jumping around in that car. It gave me quite a start!"

The landlord stopped his work and peered out curiously. "So, you run a Wildlife Hospital? Tell me about it."

He was a dark-haired, nice-looking, young man and conversed with us for some time.

"I expect it costs you a good deal to run it?" he asked, as he poured a customer a pint.

"£1 a day just to keep the owls in beef," we laughed.

"So, you're on holiday here? How long are you staying for?"

"We go home on Saturday, we're afraid."

He gave the customer his change thoughtfully. "Why can't we do a spot of fundraising for you while you're here?" he announced. "We could make Friday a special evening."

"Would you really? That would be wonderful."

"I'll have a talk to Jane, my wife. I'm sure by tomorrow we'll have thought of something."

As we were leaving the pub, the customers told us, "Of course, you know who Chris is, don't you? He's Fanny Cradock's son, the T.V. Gourmet. He's very popular here."

Sure enough, the next day Chris came up with the promised ideas. "Jane suggested a mock auction and I don't see why we couldn't have a raffle as well."

"Splendid!" we replied, overwhelmed. "But can you spare the time to do all that here?"

"Of course. The customers will enjoy it. I've asked them to bring anything that could make a bit of money."

On the Friday night, people arrived with clocks, books, toys, toiletries, bric-a-brac, plants and flowers, cakes and everything one could imagine and at seven-thirty the auction began. We felt Chris should be a T.V. star himself.

"Ten pounds I'm bid for this," he called, holding up a tea-pot, "and what about this Bierstein? Anybody offer me a fiver?" "Who'll give me 50p for this teddy bear?" and by the end of the evening the total sum collected had reached £215!

We thanked him profusely.

"Come back and see us again," he asked, "and we'll do some more fundraising for you."

We journeyed home the next day with all our charges and May met us at the door.

"Everything all right?" we asked.

"Yes, I've had quite an adventure," she said, the relief showing on her face. "What do you think happened? Henry got up on the shed roof."

"The shed roof? With his plastered leg?"

"Yes. I just didn't know what to do. Then in sheer desperation, I put first one fish down and waited for him to pick it up, then another and walking back a couple of steps, put down another until he flew down. Then teasing him a bit further, then further still, I managed to lure him into the shed and shut the door!"

During that spring and summer there appeared two photos of our hospital in The Newbury Weekly News—one 12" x 9" of me holding a duckling and a baby woodpecker and another of two young children, Sarah and Sean, from The Fir Tree School, holding Nelson, our blind Tawny owl.

Then in September strange things began to happen. A man arrived with a feral pigeon.

"I found it in the canal and fished it out just in time," he told us. "How it got in there, I've no idea. Its feathers seem to be coated in glue."

We examined its bedraggled wings, which were totally maimed.

"Good heavens!" I replied. "We'll have to work hard on this."

But before we could begin to clean it, yet another one arrived. Then along came a lady with another and a boy with another, until we had seven in one weekend.

Then the phone rang. "Is that The Newbury Wildlife Hospital? Pigeons are dropping to their death from the shops opposite St. Nicolas' Church."

We put our thinking caps on.

"The tower of that church is being restored, isn't it?" Yvonne remarked. "The pigeons which normally roost upon it must have gone to roost elsewhere and there must be something wrong with those shops."

We decided to do a bit of detective work and walked down there. It didn't take long to see what the trouble was. The roofs had been coated with a thick, black substance and we were successful in tracking down the culprit. A London firm that produced this gluey pigeon deterrent had been employed to do the job. We telephoned The Newbury Weekly News without a moment's delay.

Along came cheery, little Ron Lambert once again and we showed him some of the victims.

"Right, we'll take a picture of you and Yvonne standing in front of St. Nick's holding them," he declared.

On the 12th September, the impressive photo appeared on the front page with the headline, 'Glued-up Pigeons Have Made Miss Louise Veness Hopping Mad!'

It had the desired effect. We succeeded in getting it stopped.

Isn't it amazing what lengths some people will go to, to achieve their own ends? On another occasion, in the main Northbrook Street, poor birds were being trapped in cages on the roofs of several shops and left to die with no food or water. I called upon every manager in turn and informed him that if those cages were not removed forthwith, I would call the RSPCA.

I can quite understand that pigeons do make a mess and must be deterred, but let's do it humanely. Out of the nesting season, why not simply wire up the ledges on which they roost? I have seen this done quite successfully over an empty shop in Cheap Street.

The press couldn't have worded it better. I *was* hopping mad!

CHAPTER 14
1975

In the bitter cold of February, into our shop walked a tramp, fumbled in his pocket and pulled out a pound note which dropped on to the floor. Picking it up, he handed it over and said, "This is for your wildlife," and walked out without any explanation!

Isn't it acts of kindness like these which sustain one's faith in human nature?

Not many weeks later we received another surprise visitor. Who should it be but Chris himself!

"Just on my way to Norfolk to visit my mother," he explained, "and brought you a patient. Winston is my little boy's pet. Could you mend his wing for him? I will call for him on my way back."

"Of course we will. Have you time for a cuppa?"

"Just a very quick one."

We boiled up the kettle.

"I hope we'll see you in the spring," he remarked, as he sat drinking it and warming himself up. "We'll have to think up some more ideas for fundraising.

"I expect May will look after the hospital again for us. We'll certainly try and come."

He departed, leaving us with Winston, who was a Tawny owl.

What with getting up at six every morning, looking after the hospital and entertaining at weekends, our every minute was filled, yet we managed to keep our promise and make the trip to Devon.

"Good to see you!" cried Chris and Jane upon our arrival. "What do you think of this idea? An Owl's Supper—until two or three in the morning?"

"What will that be?" we laughed. "Voles and mice?"

"Sausages, beans and chips."

"Sounds good to us."

With Chris's charisma, it proved to be a sell-out and once again we came away with over £200.

Back home again, the months passed quickly and one morning in September the telephone rang with no small degree of urgency and I picked it up.

"There's a pelican on the river and it's eating all my fish!" It was the voice of a keeper at the other end.

"Good heavens! Where?" I asked.

"On the trout farm here at Denford Park. Could you come and catch it?"

"Are you sure you're not having us on?"

"No honestly, there really is."

We set off in the direction of Hungerford and found the man watching the lake and tearing his hair out! Standing in the centre of the expanse of water was the white spectacle of a pelican. I had taken the precaution of bringing my waders, put them on and squelched in to a depth of two feet. Then from my pocket, I produced a herring and tossed it to the bird. It caught it neatly in its grotesque mouth. I tossed another, approaching it and thinking of the phrase 'gently, gently, catchee monkey'. But I had no need to worry. The pelican was obviously used to humans and I soon reached it, took it in my arms and carried it back to the car. We began the ten miles back home with Yvonne holding it on her lap, keeping her hand on its bill to tuck its pouch up, or each time it opened its mouth, it dropped down like a concertina! At traffic lights we were greeted by passers-by who stared, then ended up with smiles on their faces, wondering what on earth it was.

"Howzat!" said Yvonne to the ducks back home, as she offloaded her charge on to our pond. "Bet you've never seen one of these before, have you?"

Despise its surreptitious feed at the trout farm, it was obviously still ravenous. It devoured a bowl of herrings in ten seconds flat.

"Good grief," I gasped, "at this rate that creature will need a bucket of fish a day to keep it alive. What are we going to do?"

"What about asking Radio Oxford. Couldn't they announce it for us?" Yvonne suggested.

"A good idea!" I replied and phoned them straight away.

Very helpfully, the D.J. announced it at the head of their 'Pets Lost and Found' spot that day—and at 6 p.m. the phone rang. It was a keeper from the Dudley Zoo.

"So that's where she's got to! I'll come and fetch her."

The keeper arrived an hour or two later in his van, all the way from Worcestershire and upon seeing her, announced, "Your mate's been pining for you, Bertha. You're a bad lass."

He picked her up, put her in a cage and Bertha was transported a hundred miles to her crestfallen lover back home.

It was not long after that we set out on another unusual adventure. At the other end of the telephone was the voice of a young girl.

"I work at Hollington House. It's the residence of The Honourable Lucy Holland and I have found an injured blackbird. Please could you come and fetch it?"

Hollington House was a large mansion at Highclere, south

of Newbury, on the Hampshire / Berkshire border. We locked up the shop, motored the five miles and once we had found it, wended our way up the long drive.

But at the top we were confronted by the apparition of a woman dressed in grey with a large hat, bustle and laced-up boots, like something out of a Victorian novel.

"And who are you, may I ask?" It was obviously The Honourable Lucy Holland.

"We're from The Newbury Wildlife Hospital. We've come to collect a blackbird."

"Have you indeed? And who asked you to come?"

"One of your domestic staff," we replied.

Her lips curled. To make a telephone call without her knowledge was an act of the highest insubordination. She swept off towards the kitchen.

Somewhat intrigued, we followed at a distance to where her domestic staff, arrayed in the same old-fashioned dress applicable to the day, lined up in terror.

"Who telephoned these people?" she demanded.

The young maid, obviously in her first job, admitted her guilt. We waited no longer, not wishing to cause any further embarrassment, collected the bird and returned home.

Next day the young girl came to see us. She had received instant dismissal!

Soon December was nearing, the days were getting colder and we began thinking about our musical programme for the Christmas season. As usual, the atmosphere in the shops and market was becoming alive with festive fever and everyone was laughing and being jostled by the crowds.

Elsie and Reg began practising 'Wintering in Winter Wonderland', I brought out the ukulele for an airing with an arrangement of 'Jingle Bells', while Yvonne spent her time gargling, warding off germs.

But one night we arrived for our usual weekend duties and were met with a shock. John and Vicky had something they wanted to announce to the customers.

"We've been offered the chance to run another pub. It's called 'The Plough' at Reading."

"Oh dear! But you're not going, surely?" everyone asked, dismayed.

"Well, it's larger than this, you see and would be a challenge to us."

"Then you are," they said sadly.

"Yes, I'm afraid so," John apologised. "We have thought and thought about it and have at last made up our minds. We'll be very sorry to leave you all."

He spoke to us in private. "We will do our utmost to encourage the incoming landlords to retain the band," he promised. "The amount of trade you have brought to us has been phenomenal. I'm sure they will agree."

But how wrong he was. The new landlords said they were not interested and were not 'into music'.

That Christmas the cheerful sounds of 'Ding Dong Merrily on High' disguised everyone's feelings and rang out from 'The Cooper's Arms' for the very last time.

CHAPTER 15
1976

In the new year, Tawny fell from the back of a chair and we found him lying on the floor, his body twitching violently in one of his fits. We rushed for cold water and doused him in the usual way. Soon, he was back to normal again—but in five hours' time, as we were sitting in the evening by the fire, down he fell again, his body in the same contortions.

Very distraught, we took him to bed with us that night but he never woke up. By morning he was in a coma and the vet could do nothing. That day he passed away.

What a character he had been! We knew we would never forget his wonderful, cheeky ways and we buried him with Magnus beneath the elder tree.

And they say troubles never come singly, don't they? That year was fraught with problems.

On a Monday morning, the 5th July, Mr. Thompson came to see us. "You remember that fellow who called a week ago from The Housing Department?" he began.

We did. He had informed us the Council had received complaints that we kept animals in the house, which was unhygienic and he had no alternative but to carry out an inspection of the premises. It was obvious that buildings dating from the sixteenth century would never meet today's standards and we had had a strong foreboding.

"Well, I've heard from the Council today," Mr. Thompson

continued, "and have some bad news. He's declared them unfit for human habitation and the conditions they demand would require such an exorbitant amount of money to be spent on them, that I could never afford it."

"So what will you do?"

He shrugged. "I'll just have to sell up. I'm very sorry. I'm sure you realise it is not my wish."

"Of course not. You have always been a most kind landlord."

When he had gone, we looked at each other in despair. He had decided he would sell both numbers 31 and 33 together which made us worry about May and Jim as well. However, in time they were re-accommodated and were happy but our situation with the hospital was difficult, to say the least.

Some weeks later we received a letter from the Council. A house could be allocated to us in St. Michael's Road, it read, but we would not be permitted to take our wildlife there. We knew we simply could not go anywhere without them.

That month, a likely purchaser came to view both premises. He was Mr. Thomas Franklin, an antique dealer from the next road whom we knew. He seemed content to buy them for a song and was rich enough to renovate them.

While looking round, he mentioned a site scheduled for redevelopment at some time in the future, in Pelican Lane. We decided to go and have a scout around. Pelican Lane was so named, because once a very well-known seventeenth century coaching inn had stood there called 'The George and Pelican'.

There we found number 18, a bay-windowed semi-detached house with three storeys, a good-sized garden and a paddock to the rear. The adjoining property, number 20 was also empty and the two stood on their own, a distance from other houses. What an ideal situation it would be! We took the bull by the horns and wrote, asking the Council if it would be possible to move to number 18, no matter how temporarily.

We also had an idea. Next day we put a table and chair outside our shop, displaying a placard asking for signatures for the Council to re-house us with our hospital. People came in twos and threes and were wonderful. We collected over three hundred signatures and delivered the collection to the Council offices.

As a result, we received a visit from one of their members, Councillor Cyril Woodward. He looked around the house and hospital and proved to be the most splendid champion we had ever had. At the next Council meeting, he informed them that our premises were clean and tidy and added what a worthwhile job we did!

But Councils work slowly and at last, on the 22nd September a letter arrived. We tore it open feverishly before we had even breakfasted and the contents were more than we had bargained for.

"We write to inform you that we are able to offer you accommodation at no. 18 Pelican Lane and the adjoining cottage as well, no 20. You also have permission to take your wildlife.

Use of the paddock to the rear and the sheds is included.

The keys may be obtained for viewing from these offices but we must inform you that the lease will only be for a period of two years, after which time the site is scheduled for redevelopment.

We await your written acceptance."

We could not believe our luck. We found ample rooms for ourselves and those patients in need of special care and there was even a conservatory. There was everything that we wanted.

We delivered our letter by hand that day, also receiving their agreement that they would put a few repairs in hand before we took up occupation. They agreed to do the absolute minimum and the date when these were completed was the 11th November. Accordingly, we hired a van and with the help of May and Jim and other friends, loaded up our belongings, dismantled the aviaries and in several journeys, transported the patients to their new abode.

Though condemned properties, to us they were Shangri-la.

Tawny and Rabbit friends which would normally be predated in the wild
Picture by David Hartley

CHAPTER 16
1977

As soon as we had entered the house, Eno was in his element, standing on his hind legs peering out of the bay-window and when we opened the back door, he scampered down the garden and into the paddock beyond, yapping as he explored every shed.

Meanwhile, we set to work accommodating all the patients next door in the twelve rooms.

"Look, I've found a dark room," Yvonne called, opening a door. It had obviously once been a larder. "This could be the intensive care unit and perhaps even a bat room in the spring."

That agreed, we moved all the very sick patients in carefully. Next, we gave the owls a room to themselves, allotted one to the two pheasants, one to a heron and set one aside for any foxes or badgers.

"You see this room here facing the garden? How about putting all the 'cat casualties' in here?" I suggested. "Then if we wire-net an enclosure outside and keep the window open, they can wander around to their hearts' content." (Sadly, such patients, the little songbirds, were ever present at the hospital.)

She thought that was a magnificent idea. But there is a law in the world of nature which must be obeyed. We knew we could never put certain birds in together. For instance, a magpie will kill a young bird and peck its eyes out, thinking that they are beads. On the other hand, a rook will kill a magpie.

The usefulness of number 20 proved itself beyond bounds.

In the frost of January, an RSPCA van drove all the way from Southampton Water bringing a large batch of seagulls. What a pathetic sight it was and the usual trauma! The poor things were covered in oil from a tanker spillage. Immediately we converted the kitchen into a casualty unit and after we had worked like Trojans for two hours, felt rewarded that we had managed to save all twenty.

But a few days afterwards, who should draw up at the hospital but the police? I opened the door to a burly constable.

"Morning, Miss," then seeing my surprised face, joked, "Don't worry. I haven't come to arrest you. Come and see what I've got in the van."

I followed him outside curiously and watched as he opened the door. Inside was a swan, sitting pitifully in a cage.

The constable indicated its neck. "Can you believe what some louts will get up to? It was found on the lakes at Thatcham."

"Good heavens, gunshot wounds!" I said, appalled. "Have you caught the culprits?"

"Yes, a gang of youngsters."

"We've seen enough shot ducks and geese in our time but swans have Crown protection, don't they?" I murmured, lifting it out. "Looks like a female. Thank you for bringing it."

The swan was too shocked and sick to be aggressive. We managed somehow to administer water and vitamins and bathed her neck gently. Soon, we came across the pellets which had reaped the damage and which, by a sheer act of God, had not punctured her windpipe. There were four. We removed them gently and then applied the old faithful antiseptic cream, Acriflex, (harmless if swallowed) and put her to bed in the dark room.

Next day, Prunella seemed a little better and was able to take a small portion of liquefied greens and soaked bread. Although her recovery was slow, once she was stronger, we were able to put her to acclimatise in the conservatory.

Then a fortnight later we received a pleasant surprise. Three little girls aged ten to eleven, turned up on a Saturday morning with a donation of £4. "We run an 'ideas' stall," they told us, "selling homemade cakes and produce at our school at Enborne and this week, we've chosen your hospital to give the money to."

The spring sprang with all its delights and two more children arrived. This time they had brought a visitor, a fledgling jay found in the woods.

He was beautiful and took his hand-feed of maggots and chick-crumb with no trouble. Then after some days, we were able to give him meat and peanuts. Because of the saxe-blue on his wings, we named him 'Bluey'. His cinnamon body was also such a striking contrast with the black and white, that each time Yvonne passed his cage, she called, "Pretty boy, pretty boy!"

With his cheeky, black eyes ringed with white and his black moustache, Bluey became quite a character. One afternoon we heard loud 'miaows' coming from the garden and someone crying, "Oh my God, there's a cat in there!" We rushed to investigate. But there was nothing in the aviary but Bluey!

As Yvonne went to visit him one day, he greeted her with 'Pretty boy, pretty boy!' and we realised that she had a pitch to her voice which birds can imitate, for they never imitated mine. (Could this be the reason why some people have budgies that talk and others don't?)

Then we heard a piercing wolf-whistle coming from his aviary and when we went out, saw passers-by stopping and staring over the fence. He had heard the young braves coming out of the pub down the road!

But early one morning when I went to feed Bluey, he flew out and was gone. We realised the time had come when he felt he had enough confidence to fend for himself and needed to fly back to the woods.

But he did not. Instead of seeking the protection of the wild, Bluey began behaving as familiarly as a domestic pet. Calls began to come into the hospital from people all around, saying he was visiting them and we asked them if they would leave out tinned cat or dog food for him.

After about a week, we learned that he had found his way to the Ladies' Toilets in Victoria Park. We hoped he wasn't wolf-whistling in there! But we knew it was time for us to go along and retrieve him. There we found him perched above the washbasins, where people had been feeding him.

"Come along, Bluey," Yvonne called. "Pretty boy, pretty boy!" and succeeded in coaxing him onto her finger. And so Bluey came back to the sanctuary where he belonged.

Several other unusual things happened that year. Our hospital was given complete write-ups in the national press. Firstly, a journalist rang from The Daily Mail.

"Would you mind if I come and write a piece about you?" and when she arrived, we found a lovely, tall, young girl in her early twenties, with long, chestnut hair.

"I'm June Southworth," she said, giving a handshake as warm as the day itself. Then after walking round with us, recording the interview eagerly on her tape-recorder and chatting all the while, she raced back to London to get her story on the rollers.

On Saturday July 23rd, we opened the paper excitedly. There we were, on page seven in an article entitled 'The Patients of Pelican Lane'. A photo appeared of us holding both Prunella and

Nelson, the blind owl, with seven columns of print and we laughed at the description of ourselves—myself, 64, with blonde hair and strappy shoes and Yvonne, 53, with long, red hair and a simple delight in the wonders of nature.

June announced that we saved some two thousand creatures a year in our hospital and the cottage next-door, adding how we felt: that you can't be with animals and not believe some Supreme Being made them.

And what a lot of recognition it brought us!

A few days passed and Yvonne came out into the garden. "Whatever do you think? We're going to have a present!"

"Really? Whatever's that?"

"A swimming bath for the birds. That was a Mr. and Mrs. Berry from Aldershot on the line. They've seen June's article in The Daily Mail and want to help us."

I did a dance around the enclosure, singing.

"Will you stop and listen!" she said. "It's coming this morning—so where do you want it to go?"

"Well, how big is it?"

"Oh bother, I didn't ask."

Mid-morning, a lorry drew up and out we went.

"Would you mind signing here?" asked the driver and as he off-loaded the sheet-metal parts and began welding them together, we watched wide-eyed. It measured nine feet by five feet, was three feet deep—and had cost £200!

"That's marvellous!" we exclaimed. "We'll fill it up right away," and fetched the hosepipe.

The water poured and poured in, until it finally reached the surface and the first to be introduced to it was Prunella, who shared it with our Canada Goose reared from a chick and a coot.

Perhaps it was June's article that also inspired two more

journalists from national, illustrated magazines to contact us. The first was a lady from 'Titbits' called Barbara Lantin, who gave us splendid coverage entitled 'Angels of Mercy'. But maybe our favourite piece appeared in 'Story World'. Valerie Ward, equally talented, came snapping away at random with her camera and listening to all we had to tell her—and on Thursday the 30th July, the very front cover of the magazine bore the caption: 'ANSWERING THE CRY OF THE WILD. MEET TWO AMAZING LADIES WHO HELP WILD ANIMALS.'

Inside appeared beautiful, coloured photos of Yvonne and myself with Nelson and another with Prunella. A separate one showed Bluey, another a baby rabbit, a rescued Muscovy duck, our two fox cubs and the last, a Little Owl.

Valerie related anecdotes about Tawny, Nelson and the batch of oiled gulls, the pelican from Dudley Zoo, Sapphire the kingfisher and of myself rowing out to rescue a trapped swan. She added that she feared for me as I suffered with angina but that I took a tablet every morning and when feeding the animals, forgot the pain all together. She finished that I had great faith and my motto was 'You die if you worry and you die if you don't!'

"Let's have a drink in 'The Bacon Arms'," I suggested after we had read the article. "I think it calls for a celebration, don't you?" and off we went.

As I sat sipping a Tia Maria at the bar, who should have the diabolical cheek to come and sit next to me but the burglar of our antique shop, Albie Ford!

CHAPTER 17
1978

It was two years ago when an unusual visitor had come to the hospital, a lorry driver with a tiny, yellow, Easter chick which he had found on the motorway! We had thanked him for his great thoughtfulness. She was very hungry and because of the usual influx of fledglings, we were fortunate to have a ready supply of chick-crumb.

We named her Dame Henny Penny and once her feathers began forming over her down, we discovered she was a White Leghorn.

Today, we stood watching Dame Henny Penny enjoying herself with Eno, trotting down the long garden and scratching for hours for grit and whenever we heard a great 'pock pock p-o-o-ck!' coming from the bushes, we knew she had laid an egg.

Easter had come round swiftly and a family of orphaned baby rabbits arrived. They were delightful and kept us thoroughly occupied, hand-rearing them every two hours with a baby's bottle of lacto. Then after each feed, we nestled them down in a tea-chest in the cottage filled with straw.

One morning, I was about to perform the breakfast round and couldn't find Dame Henny Penny anywhere. She was nowhere to be seen in the garden or the paddock. I kept calling her to come for her corn and came to the conclusion that she must be indoors somewhere. But she was not in the house and giving up, I went into number 20, laden with polythene boxes.

All at once, I heard a strange cosseting noise coming from the room where the tea-chest was, went in and peered inside. There was Dame Henny Penny gone broody, snuggled down with the baby rabbits and fussing over them, as if they were her own chicks!

There was no doubt that spring was here—and how remarkable it is every year to see the wonders of nature born again.

Certain years produce a surfeit of one particular fruit or flower, one species of bird or animal and this year it seemed to be blue tits. In six successive weeks, we counted some two hundred brought to us, either abandoned by their parents or savaged by cats and as difficult as they are to rear with their minute beaks, we succeeded in releasing forty to the wild.

Not long after, we received a visitor from Mrs. Palmer's estate. Mrs. Palmer, a nice-class, jolly lady, who owned Huntley & Palmer's biscuit factory at Reading, had often rung us for advice about the wildlife on her estate at Snelsmore Common. But this morning it was one of her estate workers who called, a Mr. Dimmer, who told us he was emigrating to Australia and with him he had a young fox called Jason. He had found him as a cub, he told us and wondered if we would look after him.

"Of course," we said and took him in.

Jason seemed a delightful little fellow and seeing Eno in the house, went up to him immediately, shared his tinned dog meat and lay down beside him on the carpet. Obviously, a house was what Jason was used to and that's where he stayed.

The weather was warm and sunny. "Have you seen what's in the garden?" called Yvonne. "Mrs. Tiggywinkle."

I looked out of the window. Leading her five young across the lawn, was a mother hedgehog and we felt sure she must be one we had rescued last year after a leg injury on the road and then let loose in the garden. There she must have found a mate, made her nest under a tree root and delivered her young— spineless and blind—and after a month, brought them out to teach them to hunt.

It was the sun that had made her make her uncharacteristic venture out into the daylight and we searched for morsels of moist chicken-pieces left over from our lunch. Together with the meat and a drink of water we approached her gently. She inspected them but refused to touch them, standing aside, waiting for her babies to eat first!

We looked around, hoping that neither Eno nor Jason were anywhere about to disturb them but we soon spotted the two together in the paddock. Jason was a little too boisterous for Eno these days, who was feeling his age but whenever Jason received a 'biff' on the nose, he knew it was time to retire to his own devices, sniffing out rabbit-holes.

Despite our constantly busy days, unless we happened to be called out to an emergency, we always made time to watch the animals on 'Magpie', the children's programme, in the afternoon. It was presented by Jenny Hanley, the young daughter of the famous Jimmy Hanley and Dina Sheridan and was classed as 'an upbeat of Blue Peter'.

"I bet they'd love Jason," I mused, as I watched a pet Border Colley and sipped a cup of tea.

"They'd probably love all our patients," Yvonne replied. "I dare you to write and ask them. You're good at letter-writing."

"All right," I said. "I'll take you up on that."

What began as a joke, turned out to become reality!

Upon receipt of the letter, Thames T.V. phoned and were interested—very interested!

They asked me to tell them all about the hospital and then promised to send their film unit in a week's time. And what an exciting time it was!

The drama began early in the morning. Up pulled the outside broadcasting van with its arc-lights and 'THAMES TELEVISION' painted on it; and in ran the camera crew to take a survey of the situation. When they were ready and had set up their equipment, they began with us showing them round number 20, with all its occupants. Next, they zoomed in on the aviaries in the garden and the swans coming out of their splendid bath to be fed. When the crew came into the house for a lunch-time break, they decided to film Jason sprawled out in Eno's dog-bed.

All day long they were with us, for each 'take' had to be perfect and when they finally departed with cheerful "Goodbyes", they assured us that we would appear on the present series in three weeks' time.

The day came at last and we switched on excitedly.

"Now," said Jenny, to her audience of children, "I wonder if any of you has ever heard of a wildlife hospital? Well, two ladies by the name of Louise and Yvonne Veness who live in Newbury, have run one for twenty years out of their own money, looking after all the sick and injured birds and animals brought to them by the public, often from miles away. Would you like to see them?"

"YES!" they shouted.

"Well, here they are."

The hospital was on the screen. The cameras 'panned' round the garden full of aviaries, then went into the rooms in number 20, one by one. There we were!—holding first the tawnies, then the barn owls. Next, we were showing the tea-chest now occupied by a squirrel with her young; a handsome golden pheasant brought in that day, a badger in the attic and then all the song-birds in their wire-netted flight. Next, we were in our house with Jason and Eno and lastly, feeding the swans in their bath, when most appropriately, a magpie flew down asking for bits of bacon fat!

It was all over—but what a host of good wishes it brought—(and even a few donations!)—from different parts of the country. It also brought a visitor in the form of Mrs. Palmer.

She had come to congratulate us and sat drinking a cup of tea, watching Jason.

"Do tell me, was he the cub Mr. Dimmer brought to you from my estate?" she asked.

"Yes, we've had him six months now."

She stroked him as he sat by her side. "He's adorable. Would you mind awfully if I have him back? He can live in my house and have all my woods at 'Bussock Main' to wander in."

We felt sad at the request but we knew in our heart of hearts that she was right. Mrs. Palmer's estate was free of shooting and a fox is a creature of the wild. What excuse had we but to allow her to take him?

That morning, we watched as she departed with Jason sitting by her side on the passenger seat of her car, looking for all the world as if he owned it!

I disappeared into the garden and began cleaning out one of the aviaries. It was occupied by a pair of kestrels which we had had for some time and I talked to them as I worked. Yvonne came out into the enclosure and heard me.

"I was telling them they soon ought to go," I remarked, as I refilled their water-bowl.

"Yes, there doesn't seem much wrong with either of them now, does there?" she agreed. "They're flying around happily enough. It's about time we went to see them all at the Craven Estate again."

In 1975, Humphry had reached his eighteenth birthday and had become the 7th Earl of Craven and 13th Viscount Uffington, inheriting the entire wealth of the estate. He was twenty-one now and we had sent him a card.

"Let's go this morning," I decided.

Soon we were on our way but as we reached the beautiful parkland, something happened which we could not believe. We were hailed by one of the long-serving gardeners.

"Do not release anything here, Louise," he called.

We stopped as he came over to us looking troubled. "Why, whatever's the matter, Tom?"

"Lady Craven has left with the rest of the family and gone to live in Sussex. Everything has changed... changed terribly," he said sadly. "The whole estate is a different place. Nothing is the same anymore."

He rested upon his gardening fork. "The birds will be shot. Humphry breeds pheasants now and has granted shooting rights upon the land."

We received the news, dumbfounded. "But he was always such a kind, gentle boy."

"Yes, but not now." He looked round surreptitiously. "It's drugs that's changed him. He's become an addict, mixes with rock-stars and holds drug parties in the barns. It's soul-destroying to see him."

We drove away, shattered. When Yvonne had recovered, she voiced her thoughts out loud. "Can you recall the words of Kenneth Banner that afternoon we had tea with Lady Craven?"

I could and drove along in silence, too shocked to think of anything to say.

"Do you think they had some sort of presentiment?" she asked eventually.

"No idea."

In October, we read that one hundred and fifty-nine lots of the Craven gold and silver family heirlooms were coming up for auction at Christie's. Humphry was eroding the estate away.

CHAPTER 18
1979

Barny, the barn owl, was brought to us in a very traumatic state. We had never seen anything like it before. His neck was broken and his head was permanently upside-down.

We took him to John Addis who examined him and said he thought Barny's vertebrae must have been defective from birth. We had no idea how he'd survived. We asked if anything could be done but he shook his head sadly. "I'm very sorry. The shock would be far too great for him."

That night we took Barny to bed with us, feeling sure he wouldn't last 'till morning. But when morning came, we found him alive and he even had an appetite!

Barny was unable to balance himself and the first thing we had to do, was to find a good-sized cage and see if he could cling to a perch. Strangely enough, he remained upon it quite steadily but once he discovered the smell of food, he climbed down from the perch, slid his head along and ate it in a most peculiar way.

We decided on a particular downstairs room for him, where we knew there was a good supply of mice beneath the floorboards and we could feed him on dead ones. He really was the bravest little patient we ever had and lived on them well.

Some weeks later, we had an unexpected phone all.

"My name is David Hartley. I'm a freelance photographer, and I'm always on the look-out for something to send to the press. Your wildlife hospital sounds just the place. Have you anything interesting that I could take pictures of?"

"Yes, come on over," I replied. "We have a miraculous patient that should be quite a snip."

"Right. I live at Kingsclere. I'll be there in twenty minutes."

He arrived—a tall, dark, slim, young man, full of enthusiasm—with tripod and costly equipment and we showed him Barny.

"Bless my soul! How does he manage to survive like that?"

We told him how Barny always took his mice supper.

"Well, I think he's absolutely unique. I *must* take him." With that, he lay on the floor, wriggling himself at an angle and after he had taken several shots, dashed off to develop them, promising we would hear from him again shortly.

David Hartley kept to his word. A few days later, a car drew up and in he raced. "Well, Barny has become a star!" he announced, handing us an eleven-and-a-half by eight-inch photo of him balanced upon his perch. "This has been sent to 'The Daily Express', 'The Classic Magazine' and 'Vogue'!"

Another unusual request came in the summer. "We're leaving the area," a man explained, "and my wife is very upset because there's no way she can take her little billy-goat. Do you think you could possibly take him in?"

"Oh dear," we said apprehensively, remembering our experiences with Lucy and related a few to the man.

He laughed. "No need to worry about Billy escaping. He's quite the opposite."

"Well, if you're sure, then we'll have him."

Soon the trailer arrived, bringing him along and as soon as the door was opened, a baby kid jumped out, the colour of Lucy, a Saanen. We put him in the garden once his owners had gone, where we could keep a watchful eye on him. But the poor little chap seemed quite upset without them and we found ourselves talking to him and stroking him the whole time, taking him with us as we went about our jobs.

As time went by, however, Billy began to adjust and attached himself to us instead. In fact, he became clingy, following us around like Mary and her little lamb.

On the Tuesday, it was time to do the weekly shopping when the crowds were not at their height and we had to leave him for a short while. Setting off to the local supermarket, we loaded up the car and came back within forty minutes. But as we turned into Pelican Lane, a loud 'Beeaaa, beeaaa' was coming from the direction of the garden and Billy's little dejected figure was staring into space.

"Now, now, Billy!" Yvonne called, climbing out and fussing him. "We weren't gone long. Stop all that noise," and rummaged amongst the bags for a titbit. After that Billy was quite happy, following us around like a long-lost soul again, as if we had never left him.

Never a day passes in a wildlife hospital that is not without its intrigues. The telephone rang just as we were having lunch and it was a workman on the estate belonging to the millionaire, Charles Clore.

"Could you come and help us?" he implored. "We've cut down a tree and didn't know there was a nest of barn owls in it. They're pretty vicious and we can't catch them."

"Oh dear!" I said, for the second time that week. "All right, we'll be out."

'Stype Manor' as it was known, was at Hungerford. We motored through its High Street, turned left at the top, drove a short distance and found the field where the farm labourers were. Immediately upon spotting us, one of them came over and doffed his cap. "We're changing this field from grazing to arable," he explained, "and the tree was in the way of the tractor. The parent birds must have been frightened away."

The huge oak lay prostrate and from its interior arose the squeaking of nestlings. I put my gloved hand inside but it was impossible to reach them. They were at least four feet away. There was nothing for it but to crawl inside and I was thankful that I had my slacks on. This was not an everyday exercise, being in my sixties and no longer with a youthful figure! I could see two pairs of eyes staring wildly at me from the dark interior and as I approached, the squeaks turned into swearing and snake-like hissing at the intrusion.

I made to grab them but they sat back on their haunches, lashing out. I seized the first aggressive, little form, gripping its feet and legs together, immobilising its claws. But the second youngster moved further and further away and at last, after a pantomime of hissing and spitting, it surrendered. I emerged hot and disheveled with the two captives.

"Well done!" called the amused workmen, eyeing the spirited, little balls of down. "How old do you think they are?"

"I'd say about two weeks. But don't worry, they'll survive." Putting them in the car, with Eno sniffing curiously at the cage, we waved 'Goodbye' and drove home.

As we turned the corner once more, there was Billy giving his loud, plaintive 'Beeaaa, beeaaa!'

"Oh goodness!" Yvonne groaned. "Do you think he's been calling all the time we've been gone?" and rushed in to calm him down.

"Do you remember Bobby?" I asked. "Billy's exactly the same."

As time passed by, things became no better and neighbours

began to complain. Then one day, we found a note pinned to our door, the tone of which was none too pleasant.

"We'll just have to find another home for him," I said in despair. "He needs company—perhaps even other goats. Do you know of anyone who keeps them?"

Yvonne didn't and she fetched the paper to see if anyone might be advertising goat's milk.

"Ah, here we are!" she said after a while. "Someone keeps Saanens at White Hill Cottages, Woolton Hill."

It turned out to be a young mother and when we telephoned her, she was quite willing to have Billy, even offering to come and pick him up in her transporter.

Next day we watched him go with sadness, hoping he would settle down in his third home and would like all his new-found girlfriends. Eileen telephoned us after a day or two to say he did. Who was to know? One day he may have fun siring kids of his own.

At the beginning of July, a distressed lady came to us bringing a baby rabbit that she had found being buried alive by children! The poor little soul was in a state of shock, his lungs were affected and Yvonne put him into intensive care, giving him loving attention with a baby's bottle of lacto.

We asked the lady where she had found him and she told us Enborne. Moreover, she suspected that other rabbits had come to the same terrible fate and I reported the matter to the RSPCA and the police straightaway.

Little Bobtail responded to Yvonne's gentle treatment, becoming attached to her and after three weeks, when he was a little better, she put him to acclimatise in the fresh air in a hutch outside.

But next morning we were mortified to find that in the night, thieves had broken into it, seized little Bobtail and taken him away. Was this revenge by the children's parents? If so, what kind of homes did the children have?

We put an urgent plea in 'The Newbury Weekly News', to anyone who could trace the offenders but it was to no avail. They were never caught and never punished for their ill deed.

But in September came something a little happier. We discovered that the anonymous 'Winchcombe'—(Jack O'Newbury, the cloth merchant)—had written about us in his weekly column in that same paper. To this day we do not know who he or she is. But it was such kind words as these that lifted our spirits once again.

SANCTUARY FOR WILD CREATURES.

'From time to time a reminder arrives on my desk; that the Veness sisters are carrying on their good works at The Newbury Wildlife Hospital in Pelican Lane. Theirs is the kind of public service which is so often overlooked, unless in a moment of crisis when a wild creature is found in need of saving. Something over a year ago and soon after I first heard of the Wildlife Hospital, I found a blue tit which had been blown to the ground in a heavy wind. I took it to the Veness' sanctuary where it joined dozens of others which had been found in a similar plight. Very close to a thousand young creatures have been cared for at the Hospital this year so far and the total number of patients, adult and juvenile, exceeds forty thousand since the founding date in 1959. The RSPCA, vets, policemen, forestry commission workmen and of course, the animal loving public, bring creatures from far and wide—one day last week a hedgehog arrived from Harrow and a chaffinch by train from further into London. All this, from two pensioners who take no pay, no holidays and who demand very little in the way of recognition.'

A little bit of licence, but still!

The two years allowed us by the Council had expired in November of last year, and we always lived in constant hope that their plans for redevelopment would be postponed. But eventually, as is inevitable, the axe fell. We were served with an eviction notice to take effect in six months' time and their prospects of finding us other premises were remote, to say the least.

After a busy day, we sat down with a cup of tea watching 'Nationwide', the daily news items presented by Sue Lawley. The programme was highlighting local events and plights and an idea came into my head. Quickly I searched for a pen and on our headed notepaper, wrote to The BBC TV Centre at Wood Lane, London, asking if they would help us.

As soon as they received the letter, the telephone rang. It was the Secretary of the Outside Broadcasting Director who said they would like to come and film us that Tuesday.

For the second time in two years, a TV van with its arc lights drew up outside the hospital and in ran the film crew. Cameras were set up everywhere again, zooming in on patients in number 20 and panning around the garden. Next, they filmed the splendid birdbath with Albert, one of the mute swans, swimming in our direction for a titbit.

"What happened to him?" the Director asked.

"He was brought to us with a badly cut foot. People *will* leave glass around, you know."

I lifted Albert up bodily by the back of his neck and showed them the web. "It's healed now, you see. He's just about ready to go."

"You're a handsome fellow, Albert," he remarked, surveying his black and orange bill and snow-white plumage. "Where are you going to be released?"

"On the river at Hamstead Marshall where he was found, five miles out in the country," I said for Albert.

"That would make a good shot, wouldn't it?" he commented thoughtfully, then added, "Do you think you could do it for us tomorrow?"

"Sure."

The next day, the van arrived once more at Pelican Lane. I concealed the miniature microphone supplied inside my blouse, then took Albert on to my lap in the passenger seat of the 'ambulance'. As Yvonne drove off, the waiting crew followed, filming us all the way to the scenic canal leading to Hamstead Lock.

Once there, I clutched Albert in my arms, took him to the riverbank, leaned over, put him in and he swam away. But alas, in went the BBC microphone as well! I peered down amongst the thick bed of reeds and Yvonne and all the crew joined manfully in the search but it was nowhere to be found. It had sunk into the mud and gone for good—and was worth £100!

But the fun wasn't over yet. The Director asked if they could come again and tomorrow, being Thursday—market day, he wanted to film us buying food for our patients.

Early in the morning the cameras were set up in the market place, taking tracking shots of us buying stewing-steak and rabbit at the meat stall for the owls, hawks and rooks, then purchasing sprats and herrings from the fish stall for the herons and gulls, wild bird food and peanuts from the pet stall and lastly—at a vegetable stall—lettuces for the swans. What a scream it was, watching the surprised faces of all the shoppers and stallholders! But hadn't we once played to packed theatre audiences? We enjoyed every minute of it.

The highlights of the twenty-minute film were shown on 'Nationwide' that week. How helpful they had been and perhaps it was this that urged the Council's decision reported by The

Newbury Weekly News on the 22nd November?

SPARK OF HOPE FOR WILDLIFE.

A glimmer of hope has arisen for the closure-threatened Newbury Wildlife Hospital, after a secret session of Newbury District Council's finance committee on Tuesday.

While discussing the problems of Cemetery Lodge in Newtown Road, the committee thought it might be a possible home for the Hospital. The suggestion was discussed at some length and in the meantime the Lodge is to be repaired.

The house in question was the old, grey-stone caretaker's lodge which stood in the Victorian cemetery and had not been occupied for six years. We had passed by it so often and not thought twice about it.

Now we borrowed the key and went to have a look. But upon inspection, we were somewhat appalled. The lead was off the roof of the one-floored dwelling and when we opened the door, we were hit by a strong smell of dampness. Every wall was covered in fungus and the copper tank was leaking puddles of water.

The accommodation consisted of two bedrooms, a small sitting room, a kitchen and an antiquated bathroom—with not a scrap of decoration anywhere and the whole place was in dire need of a good clean.

We unlocked the back door and peered out into the garden, overgrown with bushes and weeds. At the end of it was a small chapel but in front of this, was ample space for a hospital. The whole thing took on a different complexion.

Here, after all, we could be with our animals and wasn't that what we wanted? Beggars could not be choosers. We wrote to our M.P., Michael McNair Wilson, who kindly agreed to take up our case.

That Christmas we waited in limbo; our fingers crossed.

CHAPTER 19
1980

Upon Wednesday 12th March, 'a storm in a teacup;' blew up at the Council's Western Area Planning Committee Meeting—and all over us!

"An urban area is not suitable for a wildlife hospital," one member said. "The sanitation is to a good standard," while another even asked if a wildlife hospital was *necessary*!

But our friend, Councillor Roy Tubb, stated emphatically, "The health authorities have raised no objection," and this is how the meeting was summed up by our stalwart champion, Councillor Cyril Woodward:

"I am revolted by what I have heard. How we can sit here and make these comments about dumb animals, I don't know. If I wanted to keep twenty dogs in my house, I'd do it. It's certain that if the sisters had been doing anything contrary to the welfare of the animals, the RSPCA would have been down on them like a ton of bricks. There is no living body within two hundred yards of where they are intending to live and I propose we grant permission, without any more, silly nonsense!"

And it was given!

But we ourselves needed assurance that we could stay for at least five years in view of all the work to be done. There was more waiting and more waiting and finally the licence was granted. We were allowed to stay until 1985 and the move was scheduled for the 17th April.

It was the most hectic birthday I have ever spent!

Friends came from everywhere, putting their hands to the wheel, dismantling aviaries and loading them up on to a fifteen-hundredweight van. Then we drove backwards and forwards with Eno accompanying us, reassembled them and as each one was ready, moved the patients into it—all the spring fledglings, the different species of owls, the hawks, pheasants, partridges, rabbits, foxes, badgers, swans and the Canada goose, rooks and crows, while Barny and those in intensive care were shut quietly in the second bedroom. Next, we took the sacks of food, the freezer full of meat and fish, the medicine chest, our food, beds, chairs, cooker, television, radio and fridge, gardening equipment and toolbox and after a week of fifty-three journeys, all was finally achieved. That evening we sat down, treating ourselves to a bottle of Whisky. We felt we had earned it.

Our most important task was to begin erecting the fencing round the hospital and we wanted to make a good job of it, in order not to upset anybody. Once we had calculated the amount of strong larch-wood required, we went along to Smallridge's, the nearest nursery.

"I'll do you a good deal as it's for charity," offered the kindly owner and even delivered the panels free of charge.

We commenced the work—digging, cementing, fixing and hammering and who should call upon us but little Ron Lambert from The Newbury Weekly News again, to take a shot of us to advertise to the public the new whereabouts of the hospital.

Already, several people had found us and the first patient to be brought was a mallard drake. We called him 'Quackers'. With his brightly coloured green head and black curly tail, he was a handsome boy but his orange right leg protruded to the side, and he began limping around, exploring his new territory. A pond was what he was searching for, but sadly our splendid bird bath had had to be left behind. We had tried every possible means of dismantling it and had given up—and as it was far too heavy and large to be loaded on to the van, we had decided that that was where it had to stay.

The weather changed suddenly. It began to rain heavily, forcing us to retreat indoors carrying Eno with us, the lad being unable to hurry now because of his age.

We sat and looked around the gloomy sitting room, the rain making it appear even more grey and ugly and while it still teemed, I searched for my oil paints. In fun, I applied a stroke of jade here and there upon the walls, shading it with a darker green and as the scene evolved in my mind, a range of Scottish mountains began forming. Then, with a stretch of blue, appeared a loch with Highland cattle drinking on its bank, while above, in a terraced forest of firs, lurked a golden eagle waiting to seize its prey.

"What do you think of this?" I asked as Yvonne came back in.

The fire was crackling merrily in the grate and the clock chiming upon the mantelpiece. She arranged the pieces of porcelain and brass that she was carrying, around the room.

"I feel at home already," she said.

Quackers didn't take long to feel at home either. Ducks are birds which have perhaps the greatest affinity with man, being knowing to the extreme and he was no exception. At six o'clock every morning, as soon as he heard the first movement in the house, he began tapping sharply with his bill upon the back door. When I opened it, he attempted to fly up into my arms despite his lame leg, to seize the peanuts. Upon landing awkwardly on the ground again, he would bite my toes peeping out of my sandals, then as I filled his water bowl, attacked the rings on my fingers. In between drinking, he always foraged with his bill at the base of the weeds for snails, so that his water became as black as soot. He really was the most comical of creatures.

However, our beginning at The Old Cemetery Lodge was not one of laughter but a chapter of sadness. In May, a call came from the village of Hamstead Marshall from a family who had been walking in the woods. "Please could you come urgently," they begged.

We dropped everything and drove to the spot where the father was waiting. Leading us through a fir plantation, we were met with a sight that made us reel. Caught by the leg in a crudely built gin-trap was a female roe deer. We bent, down witnessing where the metal jaws were penetrating so deeply into her leg, that it was only held together by a tether of red-raw flesh. The poor creature had probably been trying to struggle and free herself for days and at each attempt, the more serious the injury had become. Alas, we had arrived too late. She died as soon as we released her.

***

Every day we took a walk through Greenham Park on our way to the shops. It was just a stone's throw away and we would often chat to the old gardener. He had a soft spot for wildlife and one day, asked us if we would like to house some of our patients in the aviaries. "It will create an interest for the children," he said, enthusiastically.

Greenham Park, owned by the Council, was a spot where patients could certainly acclimatise in a natural setting before being returned to the wild. We thought it a splendid idea and housed three kestrels there in one aviary, two owls in another and several songbirds in the third.

Back home again, the telephone rang. "I wonder if you have a tame, good-natured duck at your hospital?" asked a female voice. It was the actress, Jill Sargeant.

"We certainly have. Quackers is a human one," Yvonne laughed. "But why do you ask?"

"Would you let us borrow him?"

"*Borrow* him?"

"Yes. I own The Watermill Theatre, you see and we're in need of a duck for our next production."

Of course we were interested! Hadn't we been in the theatre ourselves? We agreed to take Quackers to Bagnor, just two miles north of Newbury, for the rehearsals. The attractive, early nineteenth century watermill had been converted into a repertory theatre in 1967—and serenaded by the running water of the River Lambourn, it had become a well-loved stage for celebrities of the acting world.

The play to take place was called 'Clouds' by Michael Frayne and on stage, rehearsing, dressed in their everyday wear, were the two stars of the cast, David Savile of the BBC series 'Warship' and Elizabeth Powers, the wife of Michael Aspel.

Jill introduced Quackers and they held him delightedly.

"You can see he will be well looked after," Jill assured us, and on the Thursday before the opening night, we were in for a surprise. As we took the early-morning Newbury Weekly News from the paper-boy, staring us in the face on the front page was the caption, 'THE WATERMILL IS GOING QUACKERS'— and there he was, swimming in the Italian pool of the theatre coffee area, advertising the forthcoming production.

June 5th dawned and Quackers made his debut on stage, not

in the least affected by the spotlights or audience, in the arms of the black, Cuban chauffeur, Hilberto, who had a taste for bartering.

The play did its run and we went to fetch him.

"Quackers is very popular with the public and an attraction to the theatre. Could we keep him?" Jill begged.

"Well, he certainly likes his pool," we said, considering.

"Then he'll become a fully paid-up member of EQUITY!"

And so Quackers began his new, high lifestyle amongst the acting fraternity and theatre goers and we hoped he would be happy.

June came to an end and when the doorbell rang in the middle of the night, we got up and answered it together. A van driver had brought another young roe deer, sadly mutilated. He had found him rolling in agony in the middle of the road, after a gang of youths had held him down and savagely sawn off his antlers.

We brought the poor animal inside, blood pouring from his head. Bathing it gently, we moistened his tongue with water and covered his poor ice-cold body with a blanket in an attempt to revive him, never leaving his side. But it was all to no avail. Before the vet could reach him, he had died.

Then when September dawned, upon arriving at Greenham Park in the morning, we found the three beautiful kestrels lying dead in their cage. The next day even worse happened. The wire fencing had been smashed. An owl was dead plus two of the songbirds.

We began a search to find out who the culprits were and learned from the pub opposite that a gang of hooligans had been seen visiting the park at night, armed with sticks and stones and had obviously fired them by means of catapults.

Mortified, we brought every one of the patients home, all thoughts of being able to house them there again, lost forever.

Hardly a week had passed when who should come but the RSPCA Inspector, who had brought a swan shot by an air gun. Its wing was so mutilated that I had to remove part of it to save its life.

We were incensed to the extreme. Whatever was this spate of torture going on against wildlife? I picked up the phone and contacted 'The Mercury' at Reading, to give the story wide, local coverage.

Phil Taylor, their reporter, came at once—an animal lover and a force to be reckoned with. Listening intently to all that we had to tell him, even including cruelty witnessed throughout our whole career, he put down his cup of coffee with resolution.

"We'll frighten the lives out of the thugs and get them brought before the courts! Let's head it with a photo of you holding the swan and we'll have it in the paper tomorrow."

His brilliant report covering six columns, was headed 'Terrifying Tortures On Live Animals. Help Us Catch The Wildlife Killers!' and was sufficient to send every bully into hiding.

The atrocities he listed were jamming ducks' mouths with elastic bands, attaching rings round the legs of birds causing gangrene and death, shooting swans with air guns, catapulting stones at caged birds and leaving woodland animals to die in gin-taps.

The thugs had flown but Phil had succeeded. No atrocities of such an extreme, violent nature were brought to us again.

We had been at The Old Cemetery Lodge for seven months now and little Eno shuffled around every day, becoming slower. John Gleason, the vet in nearby St. John's Road, had supplied us with heart tablets for him but somehow, we knew we couldn't expect him to live much longer.

One day, we found the poor little fellow gasping and rushed to his side—but he looked at us sadly and breathed his last.

We had had him for twelve-and-a-half years

Hopefully we said, our 'annus horribilis' would now be over.

Weekly News

JUNE 5, 1980   Price 9p

The Watermill is going quackers

'QUACKERS' plays an important role in the Watermill's next production, 'Clouds,' which opens next Tuesday.

Quackers is a duck found and loaned by the Newbury Wildlife Hospital. He appears on stage each night in the protective arms of Doyle Richmond, who plays Hilberto, a black Cuban chauffeur with a taste for bartering.

The two leading roles are played by David Savile (star of the BBC series 'Warship') and Elizabeth Power. Michael Aspel's sole. They have both just been seen in the Watermill's production of 'Can you hear me at the back?'

CHAPTER 20
1981

Lynette, a stalwart friend, who lived nearby and was a regular help at the hospital, was walking towards the town and reached the busy St. John's roundabout, a few yards down the road. Traffic was coming from Andover, Winchester, from the Basingstoke direction and Newbury itself and in the middle of the roundabout, sitting passively, was Quackers!

Thinking she had seen an apparition, Lynette wound herself amidst the traffic, picked him up and brought him back, then coming straight in, put him on my lap.

"Look who I've found!"

"Quackers!" I exclaimed. There was no doubt about it. It was, with his orange right leg protruding to the side and he began biting my rings.

"Well, you're the nicest New Year's present I've ever received," I declared.

When I informed The Watermill Theatre, Jill said she thought he had taken himself off upstream in search of a mate and was amazed that he was with us. So how on earth had he made his way three miles back to Newbury? It's something we do not know, even to this day and never shall.

"The RSPCA van's here," Lynette called, as she disappeared on her way again, and out we went. The Inspector had brought something we had never had before, a buzzard. I took it from its cage, holding it firmly by the feet.

"None of those around here," I commented. "Where on earth did you find him?"

"Of all places, in Hyde Park. He was brought by the London branch."

Hector's wing was in a sorry state and while I still held him, Yvonne splinted the broken upper arm (the humerus) before it became too set, then bound it with a thin reel of adhesive, white plastic called Micropore. Micropore was a wonderful invention, available in different widths and we now used it regularly.

Hector looked fierce. With his deep brown back and barred breast, his broad wings and rounded tail, he resembled a small eagle. Yet he was surprisingly tame and we thought he may have escaped from a sanctuary. London was an unlikely habitat.

Once he began to acclimatise, he became amusing to observe. If anything flew over his aviary, he would give vent to a screech like an 'Eeeeek', then sit on his perch and watch, ruffling his feathers and looking cross.

Two months later he became restless, often giving us a surprise by leaping several feet into the air. Buzzards are birds of the mountains and moorlands and he needed space. Wondering if the wing might now be strong enough for him to be released, we decided to test it. The highest point near to us was the Combe Hills, some three hundred feet above sea level and we drove there with him. Up and up we climbed to the focal point, the Gibbet, where we took him out of his cage.

Uncertain at first, Hector sniffed the air, then after some time, took the plunge. Taking off with slow flaps of his broad wings and sailing through the sky, magnificent to watch, he resembled an eagle even more. Flying on and on without stopping, he disappeared over the horizon and had gone to his freedom. It was an achievement that we think of to this day.

Our next injured patient was Hopalong Henry, the heron, who was brought to us after some terrible accident. There was nothing left of his right leg but a tiny stump and we took him to John Gleason.

"There's simply nothing I can do," John told us sadly, with his soft Irish brogue.

"But couldn't you make some kind of artificial leg for him? I mean, herons can stand on one leg, can't they?" I asked, risking being thought ridiculous.

But John didn't laugh. Instead, he hesitated for a while, scratching his head and after disappearing into the back room, emerged with a long plastic tube. "I might be able to make a leg out of this," he said.

Measuring Henry's left, then cutting the tube in half, he bent the end round to make a foot, adding, "Even if it only lasts a fortnight, I hope it'll get him used to using his good one".

"What a good idea!" I enthused, as I held Henry while he plastered it to the stump and once it had dried, we brought him home. To our amazement, Henry walked on it straight away, stomping across the ground. When a day or two had passed, he became so adept at using it, that he even stood on it, resting his good one!—and a wonderful eight-inch by six-inch photo of him appeared in 'The Mercury', entitled 'Hopalong Henry takes Life in his Stride'.

He was one of the most courageous patients we had ever had and he must have sensed the right time to come to make up for a little patient equally as courageous; Barny with his head upside-down, who suddenly came to the end of his life.

We had noticed he was not taking his food so well, thinking maybe it was because we were having difficulty in acquiring his beloved mice. But whatever the reason, one morning we found his little body lying stiff and lifeless on the floor of his cage We had had him for three years but we consoled ourselves with the thought that perhaps, we had given him life that he would never have had.

It was the year of The Royal Wedding of Prince Charles to Lady Diana Spencer and once the summer was over, it was followed by a winter of discontent.

As we were returning home one evening from releasing an owl at Cold Ash, Yvonne said, "They've forecast snow". They were right. The next day we awoke to a white blanket everywhere and it was still falling, tossed by icy winds. It scarcely abated day and night for weeks on end, causing drifts two feet high and people everywhere lived permanently in wellington boots. Christmas was spent in temperatures below zero, then to add to the troubles, train drivers went on a 'go slow'. If roads happened to be passable and car doors had not frozen up, commuters managed to drive somehow to work but Britain was almost at a standstill.

For our three Little Owls it was too much. They perished in the bitter cold.

CHAPTER 21
1982

The fearful weather never abated and a young girl brought a tiny robin to us, its leg hanging by a sinew. We told her it had probably become frozen overnight and held fast to a bough, in the same way that kingfishers' legs freeze to an icy riverbank.

I removed the leg gently, knowing that he too, could exist with just one but there is a rhyme that goes back to Dr Denham Blackburn's days:

'A robin in a cage,

Sets all heaven in a rage' and it was true. Remembering this, as soon as he had recovered sufficiently and was able to feed, we released him.

A few days later, a report came that he was feeding off a bird table in a garden near the canal. The next day, a second report came that he was feeding from another in the same road. Frozen or not, we felt satisfied that little cock robin (or maybe a female, because both sexes look the same) was enjoying his freedom in the wild.

A collared dove was amongst many that were brought to us frozen, looking every bit as if it was dead but once it had revived for half-an-hour in the warmth of Yvonne's jacket, it was as lively as ever and eager to fly away. But firstly, we made sure to give it water and birdseed.

Meanwhile, thick ice was coming through a hole in our bathroom wall from the street outside and we were worried, in case the toilet pan cracked. But when March came and the snows began to thaw at last, the walls of the Lodge were wet through—and I had to move my bed to the other side to escape the running water. Yvonne suffered consistently from bronchitis and the doctor advised her to live in warm conditions, so we decided we would put on velvet gloves and ask the Council if they could install central heating for us.

But the inevitable wait ensued and at last the answer came. An estimate for this would be a minimum of £3,000 and the result was a definite 'No'. One lady councillor said sarcastically that, "It would be heating for the birds."

We have often laughed at this. A lady journalist once described us as such—'Yvonne as 'a pouter pigeon', plump, soft and round, her face pink without make-up, her voice like a sort of high-pitched cooing'—while I could be a macaw or a jay, some loud and jolly bird with gorgeous plumage and a wicked sense of humour'.

But when the spring returned at last, we forgot our ailments being so taken up again with the usual fledglings in their scores and one we took to especially, a baby herring gull, which we called Mackie.

Dwelling in another aviary we already had a herring gull, very quiet and snooty, which thrived on cheese, bread and fish—so we introduced Mackie to him, feeling sure he would like company. But Snooty didn't! Mackie proved far too much for him. He wasn't the slightest bit quiet. In fact, he was so lively that he gobbled up all the food in a trice, leaving nothing for his gentlemanly companion—and repeated this every mealtime. We had to take Mackie out and put him in a recently made pond.

But he didn't care a tinker's cuss for the swans either, or for Hopalong Henry or even Quackers and gobbled all their food up as well.

In April, the RSPCA Inspector brought us another patient: a female fox, found in the woods at Bucklebury. Her paw was bleeding and she was limping badly, as if she had caught it on some barbed wire.

I put my gloves on and held her firmly while Yvonne gave her a drink, bathed her wounds and bandaged her up. Then we put her in an empty cage, leaving food in with her. But she was far too nervous to touch it and we left her to her own devices while we continued our rounds.

When we had toured the hospital, fed the swans and cleaned out an empty aviary, we came back to study her.

"You know, I think she's pregnant," Yvonne remarked. "She's plump around the midriff."

"I've been thinking the same. Foxes mate in January, don't they? Well, her paw shouldn't take too long to heal. Then we'll take her back to Bucklebury."

But overnight Gemma disappeared! We discovered a hole chewed through her cage, the wire torn back and she had gone. We searched the neighbourhood thoroughly and there was no sign of her but it is well known that foxes find food at night, scavenging from dustbins and we hoped she would be all right.

The phone was ringing as we came back in and I ran to answer it. The caller was from Camp Hopson's, a high-class multi-store in the main Northbrook Street.

"A swan is stranded on our flat roof. We think it must have been there all night."

"We'll be there," I promised, explaining again that swans cannot take off unless on water.

The customers in their Penthouse Restaurant were sipping coffee and watching from the window as I climbed the metal fire-

155

escape and arrived on the flat roof. There was the swan and I knew if I didn't approach it delicately and seize it like lightning, it would seize me! Having been on the stage in orthodox circumstances is one thing but a drama on a roof-top is another.

It was regarding me suspiciously and I threw it a piece of bread. Obviously very hungry, it was tempted to try it. I threw another piece, getting nearer, until I was in the right position, then making a dash for the back of its neck with my left hand and wrapping my right arm round its wings, I walked with an armful of swan through the exclusive fashion department, where the cream of Newbury's ladies were standing open-mouthed, down the stairs to the ground floor and out into the street. There, I crossed the road and disposed of my charge on to the canal.

We often recall the amazing things we've been asked to do in our time. Like all church towers, the feral pigeons inhabited St. John's and the Rector had decided it was high time to clean it out. This meant boarding up the roof to prevent them from returning.

"Oh dear, those poor pigeons are circling round and round and can't find their entry holes," wailed one lady. "Could you catch them? They have nowhere to go."

We laughed at this so much that our journalist friend at The Daily Mail printed a cartoon of myself with wings, flying up there, attempting to catch a multitude of pigeons.

It was May and I got up at six as usual, to prepare the feeds and recoiled. Lying in the enclosure was the body of one of the swans, minus its head and neck.

"That's Gemma who's done it," I decided. "She must be around somewhere and living nearby."

I gave Yvonne the news. "She's got her young," she declared, "but where on earth can they be?"

"I've no idea. If we leave food out for her at night, we may be able to spot her coming for it and watch where she goes."

That night, we took care to lock up the swans and water birds, secured the owl cages even more strongly, then left half a raw chicken outside the main door. As darkness fell, we concealed ourselves in the porchway and waited.

At least an hour passed and we were both becoming cramped and cold, feeling she had chosen somewhere else to do her hunting. Then all at once, we could detect soft footsteps coming through the cemetery. It was Gemma, padding her way towards the gate, sniffing the air. The footsteps stopped as she discovered the food and then we heard her go off with it in her mouth.

Very cautiously we peered over. Her form, silhouetted in the weak moonlight, was heading towards an ancient tombstone, whose sides had long caved in and she disappeared inside.

Each night after that we took care, just before darkness fell, to leave scraps of meat and any little carcasses which we had, outside the tombstone.

"How old would you say they are?" I whispered.

"About eight weeks. Do you remember Tom and Jerry?"

I could but I was worried. Once they were adult the cemetery would become a breeding ground for foxes and there would not be sufficient food for them. Moreover, we had to protect our wildlife. We had to do something drastic and it would be a two-edged sword. Somehow, we would have to catch those cubs before they were too old and re-home them.

Together we thought up a plan. That night we wouldn't leave food for them. Instead, concealed a short distance from the tombstone we would leave four small cages. Then as darkness fell, we would wait poised ready to watch.

Night-time came and with everything prepared, we waited

157

by our posts. At length, a little figure emerged quietly. It was Gemma and realising there was no food left, scoured the hospital unsuccessfully and then went off hunting through the long cemetery grass, in the hope of finding mice or a bird in the undergrowth.

It was our chance. As quick as lightning we threw scraps of meat outside the tomb and waited in hiding. Soon, out came a small cub, smelling the food. I grabbed it by the back of the neck and threw it into the first cage. Out came the next and Yvonne seized it and threw it into the second, hoping fearfully that all four would appear before their mother returned. With bated breath, we remained watching. The third came but where was the fourth? It had heard us and was hiding warily. Shining my torch inside the tomb, I spotted the little thing cowering against the wall. Cornering it, I managed to secure it with gloved hands, then carrying all four back to the hospital, we put them into a strong aviary with bedding and food and left them 'till morning.

In the daylight, we were able to examine them closely. They were healthy little creatures, three dog foxes and a vixen and they were romping and squealing happily, grubbing and scratching for worms and beetles.

It was August and contrary to common belief, meat is not their main diet. In the wild, foxes will ignore a rabbit burrow for a feed of fruit and while taking a walk along Speen Moors, we gathered a supply of blackberries for them.

But we needed to find homes for the cubs while they were still young and the best way, we decided, was to ask Southern Television to help us, which as always, they did. They came and filmed them in our arms for their news programme, 'South Today'.

In no time, a doctor from Reading was on the phone. He

wanted one as a pet for his children.

"Please could I come and see them?" a lady from Basingstoke asked next. "Ever since a child I've longed for a fox-cub." She came and chose the little vixen.

It left us with two, which didn't remain long. A couple came all the way from Bournemouth to see them!

"They're delightful!" exclaimed the wife, bending down and tickling their ears.

Her husband stroked them affectionately. "Hello, Lagonda!" he announced on impulse, and then, "Hello, Ferrari!"

"Tut, tut—you can tell he's a motor-racing addict, can't you?" she remarked in despair. "He thinks of nothing else."

They told us they owned a hotel with large, enclosed grounds.

"Well, which one is it to be?" the husband asked at last, while his wife fawned over both of them in her arms.

"I really don't know. You choose."

"Very well, we'll have both. That's decided."

She put them down and gave him a hug. "I can't believe it. That's wonderful,"—and so Legonda and Ferrari went off on the back seat of the car.

It wasn't long before we heard from Bournemouth again. "When they're not in the garden, they're in the hotel and whenever Lagonda peers round the dining room door, the residents give a cry: "Good heavens, there's a fox!""

As for the lady from Basingstoke, she calls back often to see us, bringing Susie with her, sitting at her side like a dog!

CHAPTER 22
1983

"Oh my God, we're on fire!" I heard calls from the kitchen and rushing in from the garden, saw flames leaping from the cooker.

Grabbing a blanket from the nearest bed, I flung it on to the frying pan, smothering it. But it had got a hold. Already the flames were licking the wall behind and spreading to the curtain in front of the partition.

"Oh, what about Nelson?" I yelled, tore the curtain down and seized his cage from behind it, taking him outside. Nelson, the blind owl, had been poorly lately and needed confinement.

Yet *we* were choking and Yvonne was in tears. "I thought I'd turned everything off," she wailed, "but must have turned one of the taps on instead."

She rushed to the phone in a panic and rang the Fire Brigade.

"Shut all doors and windows," said the Control in a soothing voice. "We're on our way."

They arrived in seven minutes flat, directed their hoses upon the flames and soon all was extinguished, yet because of the danger of it rekindling, the crew remained for two hours.

What a way to spend a Sunday!

When they had gone and we had tried to clear up the mess, I went outside to serve the afternoon feed.

"Where's Hopalong Henry?" I thought, about to give him his herrings.

He wasn't in his enclosure, nor was he in the pond. Quakers

was dabbling and up-ending, the swans were swimming tranquilly with a tufted duck but there was no sign of Henry.

"Have you seen Henry anywhere?" I shouted to Yvonne.

"No," she called, came out and pulled back the bushes, looking behind them, and then we both went out searching in the cemetery.

"Well, no one can have stolen him," I declared, "and he hasn't gone off on the fire engine. Do you think—no, it can't be—do you think he's flown off?"

"Don't be silly," she replied, then stopped short, remembering the other Henry at Oxford Street. He had got as far as the shed roof.

We got the car out and drove everywhere likely, looking for him but he was nowhere to be seen—not on the canal or the rivers—and all we could do was to ring the RSPCA and the police and ask them to look out for him.

I woke up next day, the 17th April, to a rendering of 'Happy birthday to you'. This morning Yvonne had taken care to be up first. I was receiving special treatment, because it was my seventieth.

"Whatever's this then?" I asked, as a parcel gift-wrapped with a coloured rosette was placed on the bed. I tore it open and a box appeared labelled CITIZENS' BAND RADIO. "My goodness, you shouldn't have done it!"

I had often said how useful one would be—in the car, in the house, at any time day or night, where the public could either simply get to know us or contact us in case of emergency.

"Here's the licence and the form to register your handle," she announced.

"Handle?"

"Don't laugh. That's what they call a code name."

"Right, well I'll be Wise Owl," I said without thinking.

"Then I'd better be Barn Owl," she said, with a laugh.

I filled it up straight away and erected the aerial in the car, which came provided with the set.

It was great fun and I switched on. "Hello, is anybody there? This is Wise Owl and Barn Owl speaking and we've lost our heron which has lived in our wildlife hospital in Newbury for two years. The brave little fellow has a false leg. If you see him, please let us know but whatever you do, don't try to catch him yourself. Herons' beaks are very sharp."

It worked! There was a crackle and a man's voice said, "Hello! I'm Red Arrow and I can help you. I saw him this morning at six o'clock on Stroud Green. He had a false right leg made of some sort of plastic. Is that correct? I got out of my car to attract his attention, but then he flew off."

It was obvious that he couldn't have been mistaken and Stroud Green was only half-a-mile away.

"We're very grateful to you," I replied. "Can you tell us which direction he flew in?"

"Towards the Racecourse."

We drove there straight away and scanned the extensive area with our binoculars but there was no sign of him.

But as always, there was work to be done and we had to return home to our normal routine, performing the 'morning surgery', scrubbing out cages (but never using bleach or harmful detergents) and answering the door to a dozen different callers bringing spring casualties—but never with a word of Henry.

Where on earth could he be? The days passed and we stood watching the pond, where he had so often lingered and passed the time with the little black and white tufted duck.

Tufty swam towards us in greeting. He had been brought to

us with his wing broken, by our friend called Brian Braid, the head gardener on the Highclere Estate. Now he sat by the pool, his tuft sticking out perkily from the back of his head, probably thinking of his mate back home. His wing had healed well and we felt it was time for him to go. We decided we would take a drive out that afternoon.

Leaving the notice on the door as usual, instructing people to leave their casualties in the emergency cages outside, we drove with him back to his original haunt.

Highclere Castle with its mellowed Bath stone and cedar trees, slept in the warm sun and we meandered through its estate of five thousand five hundred acres, to Milford Lake. Taking Tufty out of his box, we set him free upon the expanse of water and he swam hesitantly towards a reed bed. There, he was challenged by an angry nesting coot and flapping his wings in surprise, turned tail and skimmed across the lake, proving to us that he was perfectly fit again.

The lake held every type of waterfowl that one could imagine but there was no sign of Hopalong Henry. We had hardly expected him to be there. It was just a vain hope and we turned and came away.

Driving back through the parkland we spotted Brian and we pulled up, asking him if there might have been any reports of Henry on the estate.

"I'm afraid not," he replied apologetically. "I'll let you know if he ever turns up. No one could miss him with his false leg, could they?"

He was in the middle of loading up wheelbarrows with bags of compost and we got out and helped push them over the parkland.

"I'm just about to do some work in the gardens," he

announced. "Care to have a peep at them?"

"We'd love to."

Through the walled Monks' Garden we strolled, with its rose-beds and borders of pinks, through the dividing yew hedges towards the wall at the end and lo and behold, through a gate set in it we found ourselves in the Secret Garden. A scene of beauty stretched before us, with borders along either side, in which yellow Forsythia towered over wallflowers and blue hyacinths. Everywhere, bees buzzed harmoniously and the outside world seemed quite forgotten. We stood dreaming while Brian inspected a Magnolia.

"Hey, what are you doing here?" called a voice behind us. "This is private, you know!" and we turned to see the old Lord Carnarvon himself.

Brian walked over to him. "I'm sorry, my Lord. These are friends of mine who run the Wildlife Hospital."

"I see," he replied and raised his hat to us. "As long as you don't let the public come in here."

"What a beautiful garden," we said to him. "We have no room for plants in ours. Every square inch is filled with aviaries."

"Have you seen inside the glasshouses?" he asked generously. "Come along. I'll show you."

We followed him to the steamy Tropical House. It was packed to the brim with massive foliage and flowering plants, most of which he had brought back from his travels and he talked about them animatedly as we followed him the length of the aisle.

"Now don't get near that one, whatever you do!" He pointed out a weird-looking, tall plant whose flowers were turning into glossy, yellow-green berries. "That's 'The Plant of Death'. If you touch that, you'll die!"

We gave a laugh.

"No, honestly. I'm not joking. It's a Manchineal Tree from South America. It oozes a fatal sap from its bark which the natives used to use to poison their arrow-heads."

"Sounds like an Agatha Christie," I said, surveying the awesome thing in its benign surroundings. "Victim dies by accident. Murderer has cast-iron alibi."

"Well, I haven't done anyone in with it yet," he returned with a wink, "only if I find them in the Secret Garden."

The old Lord Carnarvon's over-strict Victorian father had spent much of his time away in Egypt, financing archaeological digs and had uncovered Tutankhamun's tomb.

But his son, entirely the opposite, cared not a single jot for protocol and even divorced his wife and married a dancing girl, Tillie Losch. Later, Tillie divorced him!

Now he lived alone—Henry the 6th Earl—in his great big castle of two hundred rooms, with just his pet dogs. Every night, he dressed for dinner in the way he had always done, seated at his long table alone, attended by his long-serving loyal butler, Robert Taylor.

"Like to see the other glasshouses?" he continued.

We followed him into another, where in its lengthy enclosure, peach trees, grape vines trailing up the walls and exotic fruits of every kind were at varying stages of growth. He watched our fascinated expressions, asking, "So you're interested in gardening?"

"Yes, we always watch the gardening programmes."

"Then why not come and help some time? You'd be very welcome."

And so, we did. On any day that we could spare a couple of hours, off we drove to Highclere, watering the peaches, checking that the heating was on, weeding or simply enjoying the beautiful

165

surroundings.

But we never ever heard any news of Hopalong Henry again.

Yet life is a curious amalgam of sadness and happiness and early one morning at the beginning of September, we received an unexpected telephone call.

"Hello! My name is Jean Rafferty and I'm a journalist. I should love to write about your hospital in the 'YOU' magazine. Would you have any objection if I come and visit you?"

Objection? Hardly! The 'YOU' magazine is the colour supplement of The Sunday Mail itself!—and Jean arrived that day, full of energy and enthusiasm. For the whole morning, she stayed photographing us and learning all about our lives—and on the 11th September, what wonderful coverage they gave us, three-and-a-half pages entitled 'The Hospital Run By Owls', which included a full one-and-a-half page photo of myself holding a Tawny owl, another of both of us with Nelson and two other Tawnies in our arms—while over the page there we were in the enclosure tending the birds, with Gorgeous Gussy, our rescued turkey, strolling around.

Jean said that we had cared for patients for over twenty-five years and were on call twenty-four hours a day. She explained that 'Wise Owl and Barn Owl' were our names on CB Radio and by modern technology, we were able to ask all lorry drivers to bring us animals that they might find on the road. We even found homes for foxes and couldn't bear them to be hunted. Louise added that if it wasn't for us, they would hide in some corner in terrible agony, be pulled to pieces by predators or die a fearful death.

Jean was also interested to learn that we were once entertainers and that I could do all sorts of eccentric dancing, my speciality being the Moochie, a new dance from Africa. I would do the Zulu version and Victor Silvester would come along in the evening and do the ballroom version!

Her article continued to relate how we had found a pigeon in the Strand.

***

"Just look," said Yvonne the Thursday after. Dear old 'Winchcombe', whoever he (or she) may be, has written about us in his column again in The Newbury Weekly News." It was headed 'Caring Souls'.

"Well, well," I commented, "never a day goes by without its events."

How truly I had spoken. I opened the paper a month later and exclaimed, "Oh my God! Just look at this! Humphry has shot himself!"

Yvonne gave a gasp of horror. "He could only have been twenty-six years old."

She reached for the Whisky and poured us each a glass, feeling shaken. "The title will pass to Simon now, won't it?"

"Yes, but it's too late for him to create his wildlife park."

The estate had passed from the family. Humphry had sold it for over three million pounds.

Little did we know what was yet in store. In less than three years' time, on August 30th 1990, Simon was travelling home from duty at two in the morning as a male nurse at The Eastbourne District Hospital, when his brand-new Mini Cooper crashed and he was killed outright. It was his hapless four-month-old baby, who became the 9th Earl of Craven.

The evil gypsy curse had struck again.

CHAPTER 23
1984

We were sitting chatting at the breakfast table.

"Do you remember how Eno used to beg for toast every morning?" Yvonne reminisced. "I still miss him even now, don't you? A home isn't a home without a dog."

"You know we vowed we'd never have another dog," I replied, taking the marmalade. "It's too much sadness, going through all that every twelve years."

"I've seen something in the paper this morning," she went on and opened it at an advert she had already indicated with a cross.

I read it.

'GOOD HOME required for two-month-old, white poodle...'

"A *poodle*?"

"Don't you like them?"

"Of course I do," I replied, pouring the coffee. "You know I love all dogs—cats as well, although we can't have them because of our wildlife. It's just that I'm surprised you didn't find another Peke."

We cleared away the breakfast things and forgot about it. I should say we forgot about it temporarily because as I guessed, at lunch time the inevitable subject arose again.

"Go on then, ring up," I said hopelessly. "It's probably gone now anyway."

But it hadn't and there we were, that very afternoon, motoring out to Common Road, Headley, not far from The Greenham Common Air Base—and as soon as we found the house, heard loud yappings proceeding from inside.

A young woman answered the door, shooing back several dogs and invited us into the kitchen where, chasing around the table, was a tiny, white pup, the woolliest you've ever seen.

"This is Brandy," she announced, scooping him up. "Believe it or not, his father was black and a champ. But we want to breed Labradors now and need to find a home for this one. He's the last of the litter."

She pushed him into Yvonne's arms.

"Isn't he gorgeous?" Yvonne crooned, fussing all over him. "He looks just like a baby lamb."

And that was how we came to have an addition to the family.

Brandy was brought home and introduced to the patients. He trotted round the hospital looking in the cages, eyeing all the strange creatures, not appearing over-bothered but when he reached the pond and a swan hissed suspiciously, extending his neck, he decided to keep strictly to the other side of the fence.

The phone was ringing and Yvonne ran in.

"Have you still got Quackers?" asked a mysterious voice at the other end.

"Oh, yes."

"And is he as lively as ever?"

"Sure! Do you know him then?"

"Yes, I remember him well. I'm Mrs. Isabel Nimmo and I used to work at The Watermill Theatre but I've moved to The Oxford Playhouse now as the Production Manager. I wonder if I could borrow him to advertise our play?"

"Providing you take good care of him. What play are you

doing?"

"It's called 'DRAKE'."

"Well, that's very appropriate."

"Of course I'll take care of him! Would you mind if I collect him at nine tomorrow morning? The photographer is coming then."

The next day Mrs. Nimmo arrived, picked him up in a box, then whisked him off to Oxford where Quackers had an important job to do.

It appeared that Cadbury's had presented the theatre with two hundred Easter eggs for a children's performance and she wanted him to sit on them, to be photographed for the press.

But Quackers didn't think much of the idea at all. They didn't smell 'eggy' in the least and anyway, drakes don't sit on eggs! She coaxed him and tried everything and when he succumbed at last, the photographer had to take him in double quick time, before Quackers thought better of it.

However, the picture was excellent, six inches by five-and-a-half and appeared on the 2nd May in the local 'freebee', The Newbury Journal, entitled 'NOT QUITE WHAT IT SEEMS!'

'QUACKERS, the drake, might get egg on his face if he tries to hatch this particular clutch of eggs.' it read.

'A resident at The Newbury Wildlife Sanctuary, he was pressed into service by The Oxford Playhouse Theatre to publicise their latest production (!), 'Drake', which is soon to appear at The Edinburgh Festival...'

***

It was late on a July evening, as we were about to go to bed when a voice called over the CB Radio, "Hello, hello Wise Owl and

Barn Owl. Can you hear me?"

"Yes, we're here," we called at once.

"I'm at Penwood and a roe deer has run into my lorry. It's unconscious. Could I bring it to you?"

"Oh, dear me! Yes, do!"

We unlocked the cemetery gates (a duty we performed daily for a small remittance from the Council) and waited. Penwood belonged to the Highclere Estate, five miles away on the Andover Road and we knew it would be at least a quarter-of-an-hour before the man arrived. But he made it in double-quick time with the poor little fellow, who was minus his antlers, his tail and even his left eye and we did not hesitate to call the vet.

John Gleason, our favourite, happened to be Duty Vet and arrived swiftly. "He has no broken bones," he said, examining him and giving him an injection, "but we will have to wait and see if he has any brain damage."

It took until next day before Rupert regained consciousness but when he did, surprisingly enough, he managed to stand and balance himself, taking a little water.

We needed special food for him and took a trip out into the country, taking Brandy with us, where we visited the kindly Mrs. Minett who owned 'The Hamstead Growers'. She always saved her 'horse apples' and end-of-day produce for our hospital and we told her about Rupert.

"So, you have a deer now? Oh yes, they're vegetarians all right. Our strawberries, raspberries and beans disappear overnight. Even though my husband erected a special fence, it doesn't do any good." She filled a bag for us with a handful of old bananas and lettuces and as an afterthought added, "I think I may have some over-ripe strawberries that Rupert can have," and fetched two punnets. "Their woods and forests are all disappearing you see and that's why they invade gardens. They even eat the rose-heads."

We went back home. Rupert managed to enjoy his delicacy of strawberries but we stopped at rose-heads. We felt they looked better enhancing garden walls.

After three weeks, it was the beginning of August and when I got up one morning and looked out of the kitchen window, there was Rupert chasing up and down his enclosure, kicking the wire.

"Good gracious! Come and watch!" I called to Yvonne, waking her up. "Rupert's frisky this morning."

"Gosh, he's like a bucking Bronco! If we're not careful, he'll knock that door down. I suppose he wants his breakfast."

"That wasn't my thoughts."

"Then what do you think it is?"

"It's the rutting season."

"Oh no! Well, his breakfast might calm him down a bit."

I called to him soothingly, then together we opened his door. Like greased lightning he bolted out, sending me flying and try as we might to coax him back in, there was no way in which he was going to.

"There's nothing for it. Ring Mark and ask if he'll come and help us to catch him," I called.

Our friend arrived in good time and made an attempt to grab him but deer-handling was not his forté. Rupert made a dash in the opposite direction but I managed to catch him, jumping on his back to hold him and he dragged me across the pond! At last, we succeeded somehow in tying his front legs together and threw a sack around him.

"We'll return him to Pen Woods this minute," I gasped and once we had carried him bodily to the 'ambulance', we shut him in and covered the five miles. At the edge of the woods, we untied him.

"Now Rupert, you'll have to go," I commanded.

He took one look at me and whoosh!—he'd gone, like a rocket into space. We had never seen anything move so fast in our lives and have never seen him since.

***

"How the time flies," I remarked one day at the lunch table, with Brandy nudging Yvonne for titbits. "Do you realise we've been at The Lodge for over four years now? Our licence expires in the spring."

"Good heavens, you're right," she replied, dropping her fork with a clatter. "Oh dear, I don't think I can stand all those troubles all over again, do you?"

"We won't if I can help it," I vowed. "We'll do something about it early. In fact, we'll do something about it *now*."

The routine was becoming as familiar as an RSPCA van and I contacted the BBC and ITV (who last year sold their franchise and were now known as 'TVS')—and both promised to help us.

They were as good as their word and using their library pictures, the hospital appeared on 'South Today' and 'Coast to Coast', announcing that Domesday was nearly here for us once again. Yet the days went by and still we had nowhere to go.

One evening we sat watching a programme on television about game-hunting in Africa and India and The World Wildlife Fund for Nature's campaign to save the elephant, rhino and tiger. Suddenly a brilliant idea came to me.

"Why don't we ask The Duke of Edinburgh to help us?"

Yvonne's look was startled, to say the least.

"Well, he's the President."

"What *will* you think of next?"

"If you don't know me by now, you never will!"

I searched for our headed notepaper and pen once again and began scribbling.

But the weeks passed and we heard nothing. We felt the Duke was perhaps far too busy to deal with insignificant matters such as ours but one day, upon the mat sure enough, there was a reply from Buckingham Palace itself. I tore it open hastily, Yvonne reading it agog over my shoulder. It was written by Major the Honourable Andrew Wigram on behalf of H.R.H. The Duke of Edinburgh and bore the royal crest.

'Dear Miss Veness,

Thank you for your letter of the 1st November, 1984 and I should like to congratulate you on the work that you and your sister have done to save wildlife for twenty-six years.

I am writing to The Berkshire County Council about your situation and wish you every success in the future.'

On the 29th of that month, The Newbury Weekly News printed the following tidings, which was more than we had ever bargained for:

'The Chief Executive of The Newbury District Council, Mr. Brian Thetford, said this week:

"It has been agreed to give the ladies a bit more security of tenure than they have at the moment. We are going to offer them a new licence for A TEN-YEAR PERIOD from April lst next year. It would enable them to have some security of a permanent basis and if they wanted to carry out any further improvements, it would help them."'

What more could we wish for? That year Lady Fortune must have been smiling on us, for we also heard that we had won a Radio 2

Award for our work and had also featured in a German magazine—and that was not all.

When Christmas came once again, an air mail letter dropped on to the mat and we slit it open curiously.

'Dear Misses Veness,

I have read in a British newspaper here in India, all about your hospital and would love to hear more about you and your patients. Could you please send me some photos? I am enclosing one of myself. My father is a Colonel in The Indian Army.

Good luck with your work!

Best wishes,

Amana Singh.'

We put the photo of the lovely, dark-skinned, young girl with our cards upon the mantelpiece and wrote to her that day.

How could such a message as this fail to fill our hearts with Christmas cheer?

NOT QUITE WHAT IT SEEMS!

Quackers the drake optimistically tries to hatch a clutch of
chocolate Easter eggs!

"QUACKERS" the drake might get egg on his face if he tries to hatch this particular clutch of eggs.

Quackers, who is a resident at the Newbury Wildlife Sanctuary, was pressed into service by the Oxford Playhouse Theatre to publicise their latest production(!), "Drake," which is soon to appear at the Edinburgh Festival.

The publicity assistant at the theatre, Mrs Isobel Nimmo, used to work at the Watermill Theatre in Newbury and had been involved in a play requiring the services of a duck and so had had some contact with the sanctuary.

And when Cadbury's gave the Playhouse 200 cream eggs to give away during the Easter season, the theatre came up with the idea of publicising "Drake" in an extremely novel way.

Mrs Nimmo said: "It was quite difficult getting him to sit on the eggs, but in the end we calmed him down.

CHAPTER 24
1985

The winter turned very cold. Brandy, who was eleven months old, was the only one who didn't seem to feel it with his woolly coat. None of those silly poodle coiffeurs for him!—and he sprang around the garden thoroughly enjoying himself, bold enough now to look all the swans in the face.

In fact, we had collected as many as nine! So many of those unfortunate creatures flew into overhead electricity cables at night at Thatcham and if they were not killed outright, were brought to us by the RSPCA with lifelong injuries and shared the small, roughly-made pond with Quackers.

Today was St. Valentine's Day and was as bitter as ever with ice and sleet. Brandy was indoors, standing on his hind legs on a chair, looking disconsolately out of the window. All at once, he gave a bark as the gate clicked and scampered to the door.

A young man was standing there with his girlfriend, who had a tiny creature cupped in her hands.

"We've found this baby fawn in the woods at Bucklebury," they informed us. "We watched and watched the spot where it was but something must have happened to its mother, because she never returned."

We took the tiny, frozen thing from them and had never seen a deer so small. To have been born so early was incredible and as her eyes were open, we knew she must be at least twelve days old.

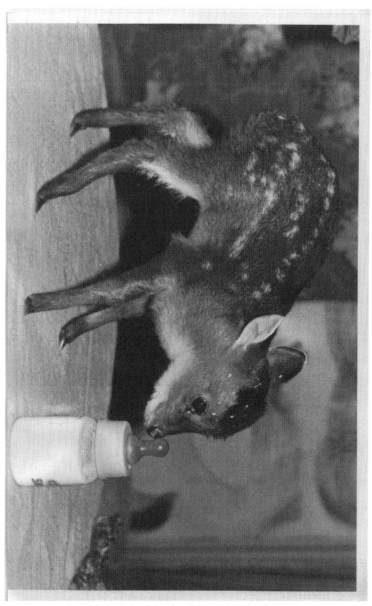

Bambi, the baby Muntjac. Picture by David Hartley

Yvonne held her in her hand. She was just six inches long with large white spots, and Brandy sniffed at her curiously.

But what on earth was she? While Yvonne began feeding her with the usual faithful baby's bottle of lacto, I fetched our book and started flicking through it. Soon I found out. Bambi must be a muntjac—virtually unheard of in Newbury in those days.

"Listen to this," I said. "These small deer came from China and escaped from Woburn Park in Bedfordshire where they were introduced. The young are born from March to September."

As the weeks passed, Bambi seemed to thrive on her lacto, taking three feeds a day, with Brandy sitting at her side curiously.

"What a wonderful picture the two make together," I remarked. "How about ringing David Hartley?"

David came that morning and took shots of them. Delighted with his 'scoop', he sent them to The Daily Express column 'Animal Magic' and the 'Yours' magazine.

"How about one of your rabbit, too," he suggested. "Let's sit her on the tea-chest with one of the tawny owls."

'What a hoot' was the caption when the photo appeared in The Daily Express. 'You would never see these together in the wild but at The Newbury Wildlife Hospital, two natural enemies live as friends.'

As a photographer, David was 'a natural'—and a few years later, captured the exclusive shot of The Princess of Wales travelling down the M4 asleep in the passenger seat of her new Mercedes.

Once the spring weather was here again, the fledglings began to come in, amongst which was 'Kes', a sad little kestrel, abandoned by his parents. We nestled him down in warm bedding but as the days went by, Kes began to feel his feet and we couldn't keep him fed. It was lucky that we had a ready supply of stewing-

179

steak, (rabbits being out of season) because for some reason, a record number of baby owls also came in that year—and they were all eating us out of house and home.

Meanwhile, Bambi was growing fast, and now in her tenth week was eating bananas, apples, walnuts and grapes, giving an excited cry of 'wee wee wee!' like a little mallard duckling. She and Brandy were the greatest of pals and if they were not curled up together on the hearth rug, were frolicking boisterously around the house. Usually, the games became so vigorous that Bambi would leap right over Brandy in her exuberance.

It was time to visit kindly Mrs. Minett again at 'The Hamstead Growers' to replenish our stocks and we set off with Brandy in the car. But before we had gone a few miles, someone was calling us over the CB Radio.

"Hello, Wise Owl and Barn Owl. Can you hear me? I've found a kestrel at the side of the road which has been hit by a car."

"Whereabouts are you?" we asked.

"Outside 'The Tally Ho' pub on the A338."

"Wait there. We're not far away and will be with you in ten minutes."

When we neared, we spotted the stationary car and pulled up. The lady had the bird already in a cardboard box.

"Oh, it's a sparrow-hawk," we said, looking inside. "Kestrels are smaller. Can you see his grey and pink colouring? And the female would be even larger than he is."

The poor creature had a nasty gash on its breast and we fetched the water bottle which we always kept in the car and moistened its beak, to prevent dehydration. Then we drove home, bathed the wound and put him into intensive care.

By August Bambi was fully grown, like a medium-sized

dog. In fact, her coat was the colour and texture of a whippet's and with every one of her white spots gone. As usual, she and Brandy were chasing each other around as mad as two March hares and were sending furniture in all directions. All at once, there came another crash from the sitting room and we rushed to see what it was. On the floor, were the antique clock from the mantelpiece and a precious china ornament.

"You know, I think it's time you lived outside, Bambi!" I said resolutely, picking up the pieces.

"Oh Bambi, you *are* in disgrace," Yvonne said, sorrowfully. "Perhaps we could make a small house for her. Then she could shelter in there at night."

"Yes, that sounds like a good idea," I said. "I'll see if I can find some wood."

All afternoon we busied ourselves hammering it together, staining it and erecting it in the pond enclosure. Then we introduced Bambi to it and she accepted it with no objections. But in the morning, she was waiting outside eagerly expecting her bowl of goodies, giving her little 'wee wee wee'. Then the minute she had finished, she began chasing around with Brandy and leaping over him just as she had done before.

It was encouraging to see that Sammy the sparrowhawk, was improving day by day and we moved his cage out into the garden. Luckily for us, the rabbit season was here again and Sammy shared the supply.

Not long after, we received a very unexpected message.

"Two swans are fighting on the river at the back of us. They're killing each other. Could you come?"

"Good heavens! We'll be there straight away," I replied and put the receiver down.

The stretch of river to which the man had referred was to the rear of the large hotel called 'Millwaters' on the London Road and as soon as we reached it, sure enough, there they were—two powerful, male mute swans going hammer and tongs, embraced in combat. They were beating each other violently with their wings, one stroke enough to break a man's leg and the staff and residents had gathered to watch.

"They've been fighting for at least half-an-hour," announced the hotel manager. "Nothing will stop them."

"We'll see about that!" I replied grimly.

I had seen swans fighting before but had never been called to referee. How had Henry V encouraged his men to battle?

'Stiffen the sinews, summon up the blood;

Disguise fair nature with hard-favoured rage…'

I was a soldier going to battle now!

In fact, I hardly knew myself. Disguising fair nature with hard-favoured rage, I waded into the river. I had observed that the victor always grabbed its opponent's neck and held it under the water—and the neck was what I had to aim for now. Summoning up the blood, somehow I managed to seize the nearest cob by its great, struggling body. Violently, the creature slashed out at me with his claws but I held my balance. Now, I grasped the back of his neck in a stranglehold and the mighty creature 'collapsed'.

As I waded out clutching it masterfully, to the applause of the crowd, I walked to the 'ambulance' and Yvonne drove us away to a fresh river, leaving its foe lord of the domain.

It was only after we had arrived home and I sat unwinding in the chair that she exclaimed, "Just look at your leg. What a terrible gash!"

Not until then had I noticed the pain or the blood pouring freely from it—and that wound took a year to heal.

But amongst all the ups and downs of hospital life, yet

another adventure lay on the horizon. In September TVS were about to film the Kennet Valley for their series of 'Country Ways' and we were asked to have a 'spot' in it!

We waited excitedly as the TV van pulled up for the second time outside The Old Cemetery Lodge and out of a large car stepped its presenter, Jim Flegg. With his familiar grey-and-white hair and beard, his characteristic cap and green jacket, he came into the hospital discussing in his inimitable friendly way what he thought would be the best to feature and how he would do the 'takes'.

What a memorable day it was! When the arc lights were switched on and cameras were at the ready, we began with Nelson the blind owl, perched upon my hand.

"How long have you had him?" Jim asked.

"For eleven years now," I replied, explaining, "Owls can live up to forty-five years in captivity, you see, but only seven in the wild."

Jim then asked questions about the food and running of the hospital, after which Yvonne took Nelson and handed me Kes.

Kes perched sedately upon my hand, surveying all around, while I related how we had reared him from a baby—and then suddenly he gave me a nip! "Hey, he's having a go at me!" I laughed. "There's appreciation for you."

Next, Yvonne put Sammy on to my other hand.

"This one's a sparrow-hawk," I explained. "When we first had him, he couldn't stand up..." and before I could finish, Sammy began letting out an awful shrieking at Kes, such as you have never heard in your life, drowning the conversation.

Jim let out a loud chuckle. "They don't like each other, do they?" he remarked.

"No, well they don't normally meet in the wild, do they?" I

said with a laugh and tried to continue. But would Sammy quieten down? Not on your life—and he held the floor until the end of the interview!

Our 'spot' was over and we were told that the programme would be on in November.

It was. Firstly, they filmed the Racecourse, the horse-drawn barges at Hungerford and then we were on, while we sat laughing again at the two stars of the show, Sammy and Kes.

A week later we received a beautiful, illustrated book of 'Country Ways' from Jim and he writes to us 'till this day.

CHAPTER 25
1986

Why does winter always come round quicker than summer? Here we were again in the ice of February, with the telephone ringing in the middle of the night and I got out of bed in the freezing cold.

"There's a heron standing in the middle of the watercress beds at Hurstbourne Tarrant," a young man informed us. "We're just on our way back home from a dance and we saw it there early evening. There must be something wrong."

Yvonne got up as well and we huddled ourselves in every warm piece of clothing we could find, setting out on the twelve miles to the little village along the Andover Road. At last, we spotted the heron in the car lights and got out. It meant climbing over a low wall enclosing the beds, to reach it.

I wondered how many times I had warned people only to approach a heron with gloved hands because of its beak—yet this time I did not. I sensed that this would not be necessary. As I crossed the ice, no movement came from the hapless creature at all and I was right. It was dead, completely frozen to the spot.

Shivering with cold, we returned to the car and I remarked as I drove home, "Do you remember that mammoth found standing frozen since the last Ice Age in Lena, Russia?"

"Yes, and it was only found this century."

"Well, that poor bird reminds me of just that."

Wildlife suffers terribly in the winter and I sent a letter to The Daily Mail which they printed, with a photo of a robin and the caption, 'Not just a fair-weather friend'. It was urging the public to leave out scraps of meat, cheese, apples, nuts and fats for the birds—and even raw pastry which they love—in a safe place away from cats and to change their water as often as possible, to prevent it from freezing.

Once the spring returned again, the birds were singing as merrily as ever, making everyone feel better. What should we do without them? The cuckoo was back on April 21st and the nightingale on the 7th May. It was good to feel the sun again, too and a call came from Devon.

"When are you coming to see us?"

It was Chris, Fanny Cradock's son. Every year without fail, he and Jane still did their admirable fundraising for us, but Mark, our friend who lived nearby and always ran the hospital while we were away, was going into hospital. We didn't know who could look after the wildlife for us.

But then came some good news. Angela and Arthur, friends around the corner, wondered if they could do it.

"Come round early and you perform the breakfast round," I said.

They threw bread and lettuce to the swans and Quackers, gave a dish of fruit and nuts to Bambi in her little house next door, beef to the Tawnies, the barn owl's beef wrapped in rabbit fur, fed nuts to Hazel the squirrel and refilled her inverted water bowl, corn to the pheasant and the chicken, whitebait to the heron and lastly, I demonstrated a most important task—to place herrings head-first on the bird-table for the seagulls, so that they would take them and did not choke.

"Just you go and enjoy your holiday," they said and so, off we set to Devon with Brandy, strolled along the glorious beaches, laughing at him puzzled by the waves. In the evening we visited

Chris and Jane. They had organised a chuck-wagon and what fun it turned out to be. On the Friday evening, Chris was the caller and the men dressed in tartan shirts and the ladies in check cotton skirts, swung to the music. When all were hungry, queues formed at the chuck-wagon filled to the brim with sausages, beans and flap-jacks—and the proceeds once more exceeded £200!

We returned home happily to learn that while we were away, an influx of abandoned fledglings had been brought to the emergency cages at the hospital and because they required feeding every four hours, our friends had brought them home and kept them in their spare bedroom, out of the way of their four cats!

Summer came and one morning in July, the CB Radio was calling urgently. A man was reporting a swan with a fishing-hook in its mouth on the reed-beds at Thatcham. Dropping everything, we hurried to the 'ambulance'.

"Oh, no!" Yvonne gasped suddenly. "Just look at this!"

Someone had climbed the high cemetery gate and let down the tyres!

A few months previously our car battery had been stolen, costing £42 to replace and we had even had minor burglaries in the house, forcing us to wire-net the front window. What depths will some people stoop to?

However, we soldiered on and our spirits were lifted when a coloured photo, seven-inches by five-inches, of me holding little, blind Nelson appeared in the national magazine 'Yours' in October and the account of our hospital was headed 'Hundreds of Creatures owe their Lives to Kind Sisters'.

In the night we were called out again, to a roe deer that had met with a vehicle near the busy Andover Road. But by a sheer stroke of luck, he had no bones broken. He was just badly shaken and all he need was time to recuperate in the hospital. We put Rudolf into a large enclosure and let him remain quietly, regaining his strength.

After a week he seemed a lot better, and I said "I think it's time for him to go now, don't you? He's taking his food well."

Yvonne agreed and we prepared a space in the 'ambulance'. But as soon as we opened the door of his enclosure, Rudolf tore out and leaped the fence into the cemetery, completely wild—and each time we tried to catch him, he had gone.

We stood watching him, hands on hips, in despair, fearing that if he escaped into the road, he could cause an accident.

"I'll get him!" boasted the paperboy when he arrived and leaving his bike, charged after Rudolf down an aisle.

But Rudolf was enjoying his game of 'he' and each time his pursuer was nearing, gave a flying leap over the tombstones and into the next.

Next came the milkman, who chickened out, saying he wasn't as fit as he used to be—and finally a passing policeman, seeing our predicament, gave chase and lost his helmet!

There was nothing for it but to call the RSPCA Inspector. Andy Bligh arrived and summed up the hopeless situation, saying he would need to enlist the help of a colleague. He returned in the afternoon and had two other Inspectors with him plus a vet!

Operation Deer-stalk began. Rudolf, aware that he was the subject of a chase, began leaping over gravestones, crosses and Victorian effigies and became even more boisterous than before. It seemed only an army lining the cemetery could ever solve the problem.

Finally, the team decided the best thing was to sit down and wait for him to cool his ardour. Two hours passed and when everyone had given up hope, suddenly they spied Rudolf heading towards them like hell in the night, making a beeline for the gate. Andy jumped up and with a tackle that would do credit to any rugby player, dived and seized Rudolf by the back legs. Another Inspector grabbed his forelegs, the third tied him up and the hunt was over.

And so it came about, that another deer was taken in submission in a van to his freedom in Penwood.

CHAPTER 26
1987

Christmas came and went. Brandy enjoyed it more than anybody. His stocking had been filled to the brim with Doggy Chews, Doggy Chocs, a cuttle-fish bone and a toy which found the greatest favour of all—a squeaky ball. With this in his mouth, he never ceased to race around the house driving us to distraction.

One of my presents was 'The Birdwatcher's Yearbook'—just published and in a snatched leisure moment, I sat looking through it in front of the fire. It contained all sorts of information about birds' movements on the ground and in flight, identification and organisations, etc. and I browsed through page after page.

'Brrrr Brrrr.' went the telephone and I had to put the book down.

"We've found an injured pole-cat and we don't know what to do with it. Could we bring it to you, please, if you could tell us how to find you?"

"By all means. Where are you?"

"Blackbush," answered the man.

"Good gracious, that's forty miles away! How good of you to be so caring." I gave him directions and added, "But have you a pair of good, strong, leather gloves? Put them on or it could be vicious."

Yvonne was in the hall, sorting through a bag of recent jumble that had arrived.

"A family is coming all the way from Blackbush!" I announced when I went out there. "What a nuisance it is that we haven't a list of sanctuaries in the country. It would help so much if we could tell people the nearest place to take casualties. The patients could also be dead by the time they arrive."

"Well, why don't you suggest it to the publishers of that book?" she asked.

"Well, yes, I suppose I could. In fact, that's a very good idea." Although we'd never heard of any other wildlife hospitals when we began in the 1950s, it was because of our publicity that there were a few others about now.

I got out our headed notepaper and wrote to 'The Buckingham Press' in Gloucestershire. A while later, I received a reply which was quite optimistic. They thought the suggestion was well worth considering and hoped to be able to publish it in their 1988 issue. Sure enough they did, and on page two hundred and seventy-five our name was included amongst them.

Just over an hour later, the family arrived with the pole-cat.

"We don't know how long it had been there," they explained. "Our garden backs on to a field and it was only our dog barking, that led us to it."

The long sable and black, furry creature lay on a rug in a box and I took it out.

"It's a male," I said. "I expect a rabbit kicked out with its back legs as he invaded its burrow. His front's torn and bleeding. Thank you very much."

They went on their way and we gave the poor creature a drink but as he was so weak, at least it enabled us to tend his wound and it was days before he was able to take a morsel of food.

"What in the world is that?" I cried on Friday 27th March. "It sounds as if it's coming to an end."

A mighty hurricane was screaming in from the Atlantic at one-hundred-and-seven miles an hour.

Minutes later, there came a loud tearing noise and we rushed outside to find that the roof covering the aviaries had been wrenched off—and as quickly as we could in the driving rain, we rescued every patient and brought them all inside.

"Why hadn't the Met. Office forecast this?" we asked bewildered, as we discarded our soaked clothes and ran for dry ones? It had no intention of abating. Hour after hour it continued, like the mighty, roaring wind on the Day of Pentecost and by morning, had ceased at last. It had reaped its havoc and was satisfied. Now, an eerie stillness hung in the air; the calm after the storm.

We switched the radio on. "The hurricane swept across Southern England and Wales, killing twelve people by falling trees and masonry," the newscaster announced. "Cars have been hurled off roads, part of the copper dome of the Old Bailey has been ripped off and a Victorian spire one hundred feet high, at St. James' Church, Waresley in Cambridgeshire has been picked up bodily and thrown across the road into a pub car park."

Here at Newbury, we heard that the Rugby Club stand had been ripped off, flying across the pitch and landing on two cars; a double-decker bus had been blown into a pony field near Aldbourne, while trees were down and three thousand people were without electricity.

Weeks later, people were still picking up the pieces. Our P.V.C. corrugated roof covering cost £60 to repair and the local

Royal Order or Buffaloes sent us a donation of £40 to help us!—a wonderful gesture.

As I was standing at the kitchen window I called out, "Oh gosh, there's the pole-cat with a rook in its mouth! It must have got out in the night."

Without waiting to put on my spiked gloves, I rushed out, grabbed it by the scruff of the neck and pulled the rook away but like lightning, the pole-cat had its teeth into my wrist, refusing to let go.

"OH, NO!" I heard Yvonne gasp and running out with a spoon, forced it into the creature's mouth, making it release it.

"Thank God it wasn't your artery," she breathed, as she bandaged it up, with blood pouring everywhere.

"Thank God," I returned, "that I've had a tetanus injection and have a good healing skin!"

After that episode the days continued as normal, until the news spread on the 19th August that just a few miles away at Hungerford, a young man called Michael Ryan had gone berserk with a gun, killed his mother, his dog, the local policeman, fourteen other people (which included some from Newbury)—and then had shot himself.

"Now it's people who are being shot by mad sportsmen as well as animals!" Yvonne declared and as if to qualify her statement, wildlife victims began arriving, maimed and bleeding for us to 'mop up'.

What skill is there in making birds that spend most of their time on the ground, rise a few feet into the air by beaters to be aimed at? Tottery-aged colonels and the like take pop-shots at the victims and the woods and fields become a carnage of wounded creatures, running around minus a wing or a leg. I wrote to The Newbury Weekly News saying:

GET RID OF ALL GUNS!

'I hate guns more and more, as over the years we have seen so many beautiful birds shot in the name of sport. Now those poor people have either lost their lives or been injured in lovely Hungerford.

I say, get rid of all guns! What a great life our pheasants, partridges, grouse, rooks and woodpigeons would have—and the deer.'

Yet there was always pleasantry to brighten our days and when I picked up the telephone to hear a film company on the other end I couldn't believe it.

"Would you be prepared to let us make a film of your hospital for the children's programme, 'CB TV'?"

"Certainly!" I agreed and along came the van, sign-written 'TETRAFILMS' from Tottenham Court Road, London, commissioned to make it.

Out stepped a cheery young man in his early thirties, with a mass of black hair beneath a grey cap and wearing denims and a leather jacket, announcing that he was 'Steve'.

"I've got a marvellous idea," he stated, with the energy of youth and staring around said, "I'm going to pretend I'm an injured bird and you both have to rescue me, Okay?"

"Very good," we chuckled, remembering our acting days and once the cameras were set up and the mini-microphones concealed in our jackets, it all began.

This time it wasn't Rudolf running down an aisle of the cemetery but Steve, flapping his arms wildly like a large, injured bird and we hurried out to rescue him.

"Oh dear, oh dear, you *are* in trouble," we exclaimed. "Come along, we'll have to strap you up." And binding a bandage round his arm, we led him inside.

"Where am I?" he asked.

"This is The Newbury Wildlife Hospital."

"Oh good. I'm feeling better already. Do you mind if I have a look round?"

"Of course not. Come through."

He followed us into the garden. "Hello—what have we on this pond, children? I can count as many as one, two, three, four, five, six—*seven* swans (two having been released)—with a mallard and a Muscovy duck—and what's this? A muntjac! What's her name?"

"Bambi."

"And goodness me, what a collection of patients there are in all these aviaries here—owls, hawks, rabbits, a badger, two collared doves, a border canary, a jay—and what's this wandering around the enclosure?—a rescued turkey. Whatever shall we see next?"

"Well, isn't this really incredible?" he continued. "All these animals and birds are looked after by two ladies who are pensioners!"

He finished telling them about the hospital and then it was time for him to go.

"Oh, somebody's left some jumble for us to sell," I said, as I opened the door for him. "Would you like a handbag?"

"No thanks, it doesn't go with my suit," he replied, with an affected voice and sadly we said, "Goodbye".

He had been such fun and not many days afterwards we were laughing at his antics again, on the film on television at four o'clock, watched by all the children.

On the night of October 15th as we went to bed tired, suddenly Yvonne sat up.

"What on earth's that noise?"

I listened. It was happening again! The mighty roaring wind was coming at 100 m.p.h. as another hurricane was sweeping across the country.

All night long, people lay awake as its fearful raging brought down power lines, road signs, crashed tiles off roofs and blocked roads. By morning, nineteen people had been killed in the land and over fifteen million trees destroyed.

But we gave thanks to God that, like the Israelites, our hospital had been passed over.

CHAPTER 27
1988

Our freezer which had been 'on the blink' finally said, 'Right, I've had enough. I'm packing up. Goodbye!' and was gone—and as I went to get out the meat to defrost for the afternoon feed, I said a few choice words. At least the weather was cold but what were we going to do now?

Yvonne was working in the house, listening to the local radio station from Reading, as I came in announcing the news.

"Well, how about asking David Hamilton for help?" she suggested, as she washed up the breakfast crocks.

David Hamilton, the Disc Jockey, put out messages asking for aid for local charities.

I fetched the tea-towel and began drying-up.

"I tell you what," she decided, "I'll ring up now." She dried her hands, picked up the receiver and began dialling.

"Radio 210," answered a voice, then, "Hold on, I'll put you through."

Next minute she was speaking to the programme organiser. "Yes, we can do that for you," was the reply. "It will be on the air today."

Mid-morning, we listened attentively. "Now, let's see what we have today," David announced when he came to the 'spot'. "Why, it's an S.O.S. from the two ladies who run The Wildlife Hospital in Newbury. Is there any kind soul who could donate them a freezer? Theirs has packed up, so what will all their poor owls do if their meat goes off, or their herons if they have no fish? I'm told that Louise and Yvonne Veness have looked after wildlife for thirty years. Isn't that remarkable? And now both are pensioners."

The next two records were put on while I went outside and pressed on with my jobs. Then I heard a call from indoors. "Come on! David's speaking again!" I ran inside.

"Well, you will be delighted to know that there has been a wonderful response to the request from The Newbury Wildlife Hospital. Calls have come in from all over the county with offers of a freezer—so Louise and Yvonne, take your pick!"

What a surprise! We didn't know which to choose and eventually decided to accept a large, upright one from a businessman in Wokingham—(we could keep the meat and fish in this)—and also a chest freezer from a lady in Reading which would hold the sacks of bird-bread, always given to us kindly by The Empire Cafe in Newbury.

But there was just one hitch. Neither of the freezers would fit into our car and as we were deliberating on hiring a van, who should contact us but The Newbury Weekly News, having heard of our plight and offering to collect them themselves!

That day, Bill Lynes their driver, drew up in their large white delivery van labelled 'NEWBURY WEEKLY NEWS AND THE ADVERTISER' (their weekly 'freebee'), carrying the two freezers, while Ron Lambert was there to photograph us as he unloaded them!

'Brrrr, Brrrr' went the telephone next day and who should it be but our old friend, the jolly Mrs. Palmer, who owned the biscuit factory.

"I still have Jason," she told us. "Absolutely adorable, little fellow. He must be nine now. He disappears for a while every time he has a girlfriend but always returns to the comforts of the house and to sit by my fire."

It was good to hear the news but we guessed she had a problem.

"You know I have pet peacocks? Well, one's limping badly. He can't put his foot to the ground and although he comes to me with the others for his feed, I just can't catch him. What can I do?"

We'd learned from experience about birds and animals limping and I said to her, "Don't worry. We find that often they have the knack of curing themselves. He may have a thorn in his foot. Leave it a day or two and see how he goes on. If he's still limping, then wait until he goes to roost, then throw a blanket over him."

"But they roost in the trees."

"He won't, if he can't get his foot to the ground. He'll have no spring. Look around. You'll find him hiding somewhere in a sheltered spot."

We didn't hear any more from Mrs. Palmer and guessed the situation had resolved itself.

When summer came, what a number of amusing calls we received because there was a *bat* around! People even rang from as far away as Slough and places around London.

"There's one hanging up in the corner of our room. What shall I do?" one man asked. "I don't want any harm to come to it but my wife is petrified."

I think they must think of Dracula.

We tried to convince people that if a bat suddenly appeared in their house, it wouldn't do any harm. The least it would do would be to give them a little nip. The easiest way to remove it, was simply to cover it with a duster, then pick it up and put it out of the window.

Then there was the time when Yvonne answered the phone to a lady saying she had a snake in her bath.

"Has it a 'V' on its head?" she asked her.

"Yes."

"Then, that's an adder. *We* don't want it."

We had actually seen a programme on the television about snakes and rats coming up the toilet!

Many people were also often concerned about birds flying into their French windows and killing themselves. We told them to paste silhouettes of hawks on the inside. This frightened the birds enough to keep them away.

It was late on a warm, June day and having done all our chores, we were relaxing for a few minutes in a deckchair. Suddenly the doorbell rang and I got up to answer it. A lady stood there with a swift, in a box.

"I've just returned from holiday and brought it on the train with me from Manchester," she told me. "The poor thing was on the ground. It couldn't fly."

"Thank you very much," I said politely, although I doubted if there was anything wrong with it. Swifts live in the air and even mate in the air—and have such short legs tucked under their bodies, that if they are grounded, they find it very difficult to take off again. Once she was out of earshot, I threw it into the air and away it soared. What she would have said if she'd known, I hardly dare think!

Swallows and house-martins are very similar and as we anticipated, throughout June, July and August our hands became full with the fledglings which had fallen out of their nests. We had to be the parents to teach them to fly before the migration period. We picked them up, threw them a little way into the air and caught them time and time again until at last, as if by magic, they were away.

Migratory birds will not survive the winter and whenever one came in late, we had to work swiftly to enable it to fly again. A female cuckoo arrived with a broken wing. How like a hawk she was, with her barred, brown plumage! We examined the 'fore-arm'. It was a clean break and bless the inventor of Superglue! Using this and binding it with Micropore to hold it, the onerous six to eight weeks' healing time was reduced to a minute. But we gave her time to recover from her shock, then taking her to the beech woods, we watched, our hearts in our mouth. Suddenly she was away, up into the trees—and how rewarding it was to think that God willing, in a month or two's time, she would be safely back in South Africa.

We were animal crackers. At least, that is what the dear kind Winchcombe thought about us in his or her column in The Newbury Weekly News on the 16th October:

IN GOOD COMPANY

'Animals crackers they may be but Louise and Yvonne Veness and their Newbury Wildlife Hospital, were deservedly included in another Telegraph feature on Britain's animal rescue organisations. Their undisputed dedication to the welfare of the real living, breathing kind of wildlife over thirty years, was mentioned alongside such famous national and international groups as the RSPCA and PDSA, with the two Newbury pensioners still providing a service twenty-four hours a day, every day of the year.

Soon Christmas was nearing and we received a present we had not bargained for. Just as everybody was about to forget their ailments and celebrate the happy season, Edwina Currie, the Junior Minister of Health, thought she would scare the living daylights out of people by announcing in Parliament that 'most of the egg production in this country sadly is now infected with Salmonella'.

The effect this had was stupendous. The alarm swept the country and egg sales became non-existent. Not that we could abide deep litter and battery houses in the least but we were aghast at the millions of chickens that had to be slaughtered overnight.

"Can Edwina Currie please tell me how I am supposed to ice my Christmas cake?" asked one cryptic housewife. The answer was to use powdered egg—and as a result, for 'snow' on the cake we all got 'sludge'.

Then, out of the window we saw John Evans, our RSPCA Inspector, arriving in his van. "Would you like some chickens? Come and have a look."

We went out to see them. They were Rhode Island Reds which some owner of a smallholding had left to starve—and he had as many as twenty-three.

"We shall be only too delighted," we said, took them in and gave them the food and freedom which our own chicken shared.

In the spring we were rewarded. As sure as eggs are eggs, they had grown into healthy, happy birds.

CHAPTER 28
1989

No one could believe how abnormal the winter was! Hedgehogs had not even hibernated and as we drove out into the country in early February, spring lambs were gambolling happily in a field, while a mallard was crossing the road with her brood of ducklings seven weeks early. Dandelions flaunted their mass of yellow along the verges, while dog's mercury and white dead nettle, not due 'till April, filled the woods.

Our hands were soon full with fledglings born out of season and then a baby fawn was brought to us very ill, which had been run over. Both her back legs were broken, and so we took her to John Gleason.

She was a dear little thing. John said he would set them and spent one-and-a-half hours tending to her, performing micro-surgery. But alas, the shock had been too much for her and by morning she had died.

"After all my hard work!" he said, sadly.

Still the lovely weather was continuing. Cowslips were fully out and blue speedwells covered the meadows. Instead of the usual cold, wet Easter Sunday, on the 26th March people spent it basking in the sunshine. As we took a drive out to nearby Inkpen, we found one farmer had even shorn his sheep!

When we returned and inspected the emergency cages, we heard pitiful cries coming from somewhere but there was nothing in sight. It continued plaintively and Yvonne crawled on her knees and began searching underneath the cages.

"I don't believe it!" she exclaimed.

In a box right at the back, she had found four tiny kittens still blind. "Who could have done this?" she said angrily. "If we hadn't found them, they would have died."

People had left cats and puppies on more than one occasion but not that young and never hidden. But we reared them for six weeks and then found homes for them.

By the 24th May the temperature had reached twenty-nine degrees (eight-four Fahrenheit) in the south. We were truly experiencing a Mediterranean climate. June came, rising to thirty-one degrees (eighty-eight Fahrenheit) and as we sat under the covered enclosure in the shade, hedgehogs appeared in the daytime looking for water, then remained for at least half-an-hour sitting beside us. It was amusing to see people walking past in next-to-nothing despite their paunches—and on the radio it said that topless beaches were doing the best trade ever known.

Then, when everyone was loving all the bliss, the media gave us a rude awakening. 'The Greenhouse Effect' they told us, is being brought about by the world polluting the air. The ozone layers in the atmosphere can cause skin cancer and the ice in the Arctic is melting at such an alarming rate, that within a few decades we will become a desert. We felt ashamed to admit that we were enjoying it!

In July, the tar was melting on the roads and the creosote oozing from the telegraph poles in temperatures of thirty-three degrees (ninety-one Fahrenheit). Rivers were drying up and one day, as we stood looking over a bridge at Pangbourne, we wondered what queer creature was heading towards us. It was a large fish, swimming with its back out of the water! Hosepipes were being banned in the Thames and Severn areas, Wales and the West Country, while in Cumbria there was such a drought that it was made an offence to use water at certain times of the day.

There were heath fires, trees were dying and the cattle had no grass to eat. Wheat was over-ripe, while one farmer on the Ridgeway had ploughed his field and grown winter barley.

"Just look at this photo," I said, as I opened 'The Daily Express' in the morning. It showed the earth—a mass of cracks rather like crazy-paving with the caption, 'Our green and pleasant land'. We British were just not used to it, while Brandy and Bambi, with no urge to chase around at all, lay gasping under a bush.

Then, little Bambi went entirely off her food.

"She's shivering—in this heat!" Yvonne exclaimed.

"She probably had a tummy upset. Ate too many nuts yesterday," I said, soothingly. "Let's put her to bed and leave her quietly," and I fetched a blanket.

Straight afterwards, we were called out to an emergency and when we returned, we heard pitiful cries coming from the direction of the pond.

"It's Bambi!" we both cried in a panic and rushed over. There she was, lying with her body half in the water and we pulled her out, comforting her. Too late, we realised the signs. She had had a heart attack just like Eno and died in our arms.

Poor dear little Bambi! We buried her near her house and couldn't speak of her for weeks. We had been allowed to enjoy her for a mere four-and-a-half years.

Then something strange happened. A beautiful jay was brought to us with an injured foot but despite her ailment, her appetite was good and we fed her regularly on diced stewing-steak. But after a few days, her tail feathers began dropping out and then all her other feathers almost overnight, until she looked like a round, downy ball. One would never have recognised her as a jay.

We were experienced enough to know by now that if a bird did not feather properly, it was usually wrong feeding. But we had only given her beef for human consumption, so how could that be?

We recalled that a blind owl which we had had in the last year had sat with his head in the air, his eyes rolling in a terrifying way, while two other Tawnies had died mysteriously and all of them fed on beef.

Now a news item caused us to think hard. This month, June, Parliament had ordered an offal ban on slaughtered cows, because they were contacting B.S.E. (or Mad Cow Disease), the symptom of which was 'eye rolling'.

Was it possible for other animals to contact B.S.E? By sheer chance, we found out years later in the Daily Mail's 'Night and Day' Magazine, that nine other species of animals had also died of B.S.E.—namely cats, cheetahs, goats, pigs, antelopes, marmosets, mink, mice and sheep.

The summer passed slowly by. The Met. Office recorded that this year had been the driest for seventy-nine years and at the end of September, the swallows and martins were still with us, mistaking the seasons and flying high in a sky that gradually turned to a vivid, red sunset.

But all was not idyllic. Disturbing things commenced to occur of a different nature, which began with a call on our CB Radio.

"Hello, Wise Owl and Barn Owl. I've found an injured barn owl in a field where I live. It's been shot in the breast."

"Where are you?" we replied to the horrifying news. The beautiful, rare barn owls were protected by law, there being only five hundred pairs in the whole country.

"Just beyond Hungerford."

"Right, we'll come and fetch it."

We drove out there with no loss of time and collected the lovely, white and fawn creature, its breathing laboured and with only an hour left to live.

Then one by one, four others were brought to us, also shot, plus their abandoned young,

I contacted the RSPB and the national press and on Friday November 10th, Fiona Moony of 'The Daily Express' wrote a dramatic illustrated article to shock the nation, entitled 'BARN OWL BUTCHER HUNT. A Trigger-Happy Killer Targets Protected Birds.'

As a result of this, a mysterious phone call was made to our hospital. It was a woman's voice and she revealed, "I am not prepared to give you my name but I can tell you which gamekeeper is shooting the barn owls."

Like lightning, I seized a pen and jotted it down. The thug was in charge of an estate between Hungerford and Froxfield.

Straightaway I sent our RSPCA Inspector out there to investigate but alas, he could do nothing without proof. He did not possess a witness and the fellow was cunning enough not to be caught in the act. If only the woman had had the courage to speak up! The culprit would have been liable for a fine of up to £2,000.

However, at least we felt comforted by the fact that no shot barn owls were ever brought to us again.

CHAPTER 29
1990

"Good grief, the wind's getting up a bit, isn't it?" we remarked, on a peaceful Thursday afternoon of the 25th January. Doors were banging and windows were rattling restlessly, then "Whatever's *that*?" Yvonne asked suddenly.

A crash had come from the street and she went to the window to look out. "Oh, it's people's wheely-bins. They've been hurled over and rubbish is everywhere."

We opened the back door. The noise was building up steam and rushing and grabbing all the spare cages we could lay our hands on, we rescued patients and dashed indoors.

Soon, the mighty roaring wind came again as on the Day of Pentecost, this time travelling between one hundred to one-hundred-and-thirty miles per hour. Little Bambi's house was torn apart, while aviaries began to sway.

Great ripping noises proceeded from the cemetery as branches split off, followed by a fearful crash as one tree, a hundred years old, was uprooted and fell heavily over the iron railings, blocking the Newtown Road. Thank God that no cars or people were passing underneath.

We hid indoors, waiting for the devastation to end. It continued until about three o'clock and by then, the hurricane had done its worst. The Highclere Estate resembled a battlefield, with the three hundred old cedars and limes hurled to the ground. Dear old Lord Carnarvon, the 6th Earl, was dead now but if he had seen his parkland, he would have been heartbroken.

At Hamstead Marshall and all around, barely a road was passable for fallen trees. It was the worst hit area in Berkshire.

Such had been the strength of the hurricane that a plane parked at White Waltham Airfield near Maidenhead, had been lifted into the air like an Airfix model, then soared over the top of two rows of bungalows and smashed into a garden!

Then, we were told that the hurricane was due to return, with flooding expected! And it did—twelve days later. It swept through the southern counties at ninety miles per hour but indomitable householders living near a river, had prepared for the onslaught by blocking their doors with sandbags.

Weeks later when electricity, telephones and normality were restored, schoolchildren at Tadley raised £400 for us and provided a beautiful, large aviary. What kindness! Then they invited us to visit them to be photographed for the press.

As extraordinary as all the battering which Mother Nature had given us, was the spring which followed, as exceptional as 1989. Our first fledgling was a blackbird as early as March and loads of fluffy, Mallard ducklings. We tried to instil into people that if they found a fledgling, nine times out of ten its parents would not be far away and they could look after it far better than humans. "Unless you're absolutely sure, do leave it where you found it," we begged.

Sometimes people found wildlife and didn't know how to look after it. "Always look up the book and check what its diet and habitat are," we taught them. "It could be a seed-eater, a meat-eater (which includes insects), a fish-eater or a vegetarian."

We often answered the phone, of course, to distressed people who said there was an injured creature in their neighbourhood and they just couldn't catch it. "Have you a large fishing-net, or one that you could borrow?" we asked them. "You'll find this a simple method."

One glorious, spring day, we took some respite and drove out to the Combe Hills. Once we had reached the country, suddenly I put my foot on the brake. In the middle of the road was a family of stoats—the father in front, the six kits behind in a row and the mother, lighter built than the male, following at the rear. Their red-brown coats and cream underparts, their tails terminating in a black spot and the kits just a slightly lighter colour, formed a beautiful spectacle as they walked along. We followed them slowly for more than three hundred yards and then they turned off into a hedgerow.

How many folks know that those six kits would have been conceived during the summer before and the embryos remained dormant in their mother for as long as two-hundred-and-eighty days until the warm temperature returned? This had triggered off their growth again for another three to four weeks, so that they were born when their diet of rabbits, mice and birds was in plentiful supply. Nature is wonderful indeed.

In fact, the warm weather had brought out all kinds of creatures and we stopped short, to find a mole on the verge in broad daylight! We picked the little, blind furry creature up and it did not demur. "What are you doing here?" we asked, examining its webbed feet and strong snout for burrowing through its earthly existence. How often did one have the chance to see a mole? Then carefully, we put it into the neighbouring meadow and watched amazed, as it swam across the river!

One has to have one's eyes peeled when motoring in the country but sad to say, some townies consider it a race-track, driving at reckless speeds, killing anything that strays from the hedgerows or woods. Pheasants in the road that are brought up in pens become bewildered and run firstly in one direction, then another. Squirrels are flattened and at night, also hedgehogs and rabbits are blinded by the car lights.

The spring turned into summer with the hot weather continuing and the temperature rising even higher than before, reaching a staggering thirty-seven degrees (ninety-nine Fahrenheit) on August 3rd. What need had we British to take holidays on the Riviera? We basked in luxury in our own gardens.

Yet despite all the heat, people were still using weedkillers. A lady brought a sick, collared dove to our door and when Yvonne opened its mouth to reveal parched blackness inside, she guessed the trouble. "Just watch," she said and as soon as she gave it a drink of water, the poor thing died immediately, a sure way to test poisoning.

Don't gardeners ever read the contents? If it contains Paraquat or Diquat, it can be a deadly killer to wildlife and pets. Slug pellets can be equally as toxic. Hedgehogs and birds brought to us having eaten the slugs suffer diarrhoea, a bad condition, with moulting in the birds and each dies a slow painful death.

This year, we had had two kestrels in, in the last stages of poisoning. We administered Johnson's Avon Mixture and Kaogel as swiftly as we could but it was too late to save them, and we always recall how a sparrowhawk which seemed all right one minute standing in its cage and upon having a drink of water, falling 'flop', with its feet in the air, dead.

And how careless people can be, too. They leave plastic can-rings (those in sets of four) strewn around, so dangerous to wildlife like ducks, who can strangle themselves with them when foraging for food. Then, one finds discarded polythene bags and even black dustbin bags, allowing creatures to crawl into them and suffocate. Tiny animals like shrews, can also creep into beer cans and bottles, becoming wedged and starving to death—while as for the quantity of shattered glass lying everywhere, how selfish can folk become to harm not just the wildlife but their own children and pets?

As the days passed, on one such sunny August afternoon we were preparing the feeds. Rabbits were in season now which was helpful, although sprats would not be in until the end of the month and we were having to substitute with chopped-up coley for the sea birds.

As I was grating up the cheese for the song birds, Yvonne was speaking to someone on the telephone. A man was saying he had a bird down his chimney and was asking if we could come and get it out from behind his gas fire. I heard her reply, "How do you think *we* can get it out? You had better call the Gas Board!"

I began tearing up the lettuces. "I hope you told him to put a cowl on his chimney-pot to prevent a bird getting down there again?" I asked. "It would also solve the problem of jackdaws nesting in them, if everyone did that."

The beautiful summer began to wane at last and once again we felt guilty mourning the disappearing 'Greenhouse Effect'— for the winter was approaching with its miserable cold. We returned to our woollies and warm boots, weathering the dark mornings and nights.

However, Christmas was always there to cheer everyone up and we sat by the fireside on the Saturday evening afterwards— two old people, reminiscing on past times. I would be seventy-nine this year and Yvonne sixty-nine.

We had first met each other after the war. I had served in the Air Force and Yvonne in the Army, as chauffeur to General Auchinleck, and even then there had been a great community spirit and social life, in which we had both joined.

But those were the days, we said, when we were on the stage, those were the days when we played in 'The Cooper's Arms' on New Year's Eve, when we were on television, saw a U.F.O.... We had had our sad times and good times as well.

"Do you remember dear Inspector Brian?" I asked. "Wonderful man and such a help to us, wasn't he? How we missed him when he left Newbury."

"But he didn't stay in Northumberland very long, did he? We heard that the icy, cold, east winds were affecting his wife, Betty's health and so he had moved to a post in Cornwall."

Eight years afterwards, we had received the shattering news that Brian had been drowned while sailing his yacht at Blackpool Sands in Devon. What a waste of talent it was and what a loss to the world.

Suddenly, Brandy, who had been lying at Yvonne's feet, decided to get up and walk towards Nelson, the blind owl, perched on the back of a chair. Nelson was instantly aware of him and rotated his head in his direction at two-hundred-and-seventy degrees, characteristic of owls. We had had Nelson for over seventeen years now.

It was a hint that it was feed-time and I fetched Brandy's bowl of biscuits and a dead mouse from the pet-shop, for Nelson.

"Watch this!" I said, as I gave Nelson his and in the typical way of owls, he took it head-first, swallowed it whole with the tail hanging out, then gave a gulp and the whole lot had gone. Owls never failed to amuse us.

Once Brandy had wolfed all his, he returned to Yvonne's feet. She was browsing through a book that she had been given for Christmas and asked, "How do you like this?—from 'The Song of Hiawatha'."

"Read it to me," I said.

She began:

"When he heard the owls at midnight,
Hooting, laughing in the forest,
What is that? he cried in terror;
What is that? he said, 'Nokomis?'
And the good Nokomis answered;
That is but the owl and owlet,
Talking in their native language,
Talking, scolding at each other.
Then the little Hiawatha
Learned of every bird its language,
Learned their names and all their secrets,
How they built their nests in Summer,
Where they hid themselves in Winter,
Talked with them whene'er he met them,
Called them 'Hiawatha's Chickens'.
Of all beasts he learned the language,
Learned their names and all their secrets,
How the beavers built their lodges,
Where the squirrels hid their acorns,
How the reindeer ran so swiftly,
Why the rabbit was so timid,
Talked with them whene'er he met them,
Called them 'Hiawatha's Brothers'."

"That's us, isn't it?" I commented.

"Yes. Just fancy. We've been looking after wildlife for thirty-three years now. Ours would make quite a story, wouldn't it? Why don't you write it some day?"

"Where would I begin?" I murmured.

"With Percy the pigeon in the Strand, of course."

"And how would it end?"

"I haven't thought yet. All I know at the moment is that we're in for another of those dreadful hurricanes. The weatherman was right this time. Have we locked all the animals away safely?"

We went out to double-check. They were as safe as possible, and we rushed indoors before the gale began. The wind was getting up and Brandy began to growl. This time it was screaming in from the Atlantic, the length of the west coast at eighty-five miles per hour and bringing the rains with it. The electricity flashed off and on and we raced to get candles and make ourselves a cup of tea, before it disappeared altogether.

After two hours, the hurricane quietened down a little and someone was knocking at the window.

"What imbecile can be out in this weather?" we asked and together, we went out in the darkness, calling "Who is it?"

It was some friends from Shalbourne, a village the far side of Hungerford and we unlocked the cemetery gates.

"Come in! What *have* you got there?"

"This little creature was blown into our doorway," they announced. "It's still a bit stunned and we thought we'd better bring it to you."

In her hands, Sally had a black and white bird, six-and-a-half inches long and beneath its downy, white bib could be seen its original, black summer coat.

"It must be miles off course," I decided. "It's in the icy northern hemisphere that birds need to change their colours. But whatever is it?"

Its tiny black feet were webbed and were the only clue. It was a sea or waterbird and its diet must be fish. But we had none. Our gulls and herons had gone. Then we remembered a tin of sardines in the cupboard.

Firstly, we administered water and when it had recovered, we hand-fed it. But we still didn't know what it was. I scanned through The Reader's Digest 'Book of British Birds' and couldn't find it, then finally through the back, headed 'List of Rare Birds—Visitors from the Arctic'. There it was—a Little Auk, bred in the brief Arctic summer on the icefloes of Spitzbergen, a small island to the east of Greenland. An expert swimmer and diver, in the fierce Arctic winter it ventured south to the Shetlands.

In the morning, we rang The Newbury Weekly News but before little Ron Lambert had arrived, it died, obviously suffering from brain damage. But I sat it in the palm of my hand and he photographed it, as if it were alive.

It was the pièce de résistance.

Never would we see anything so rare at our hospital again.

The little auk which paid an unscheduled visit to Shalbourne

● The recent high winds have also harmed wildlife. An unusual bird, a little auk, normally only found on the ice floes in the most northern parts of Europe, was discovered on Saturday sheltering in a doorway in Shalbourne. It was thought the bird had been blown there by high winds.

It was taken to Newbury Wildlife Hospital, in Newtown Road, where it later died despite attempts to save it by feeding it chopped fish and meat.